Love Bade Me Welcome

Love Bade Me Welcome

Drawing Nearer to God with the Poems of George Herbert

SUZANNE McDONALD

CASCADE *Books* • Eugene, Oregon

LOVE BADE ME WELCOME
Drawing Nearer to God with the Poems of George Herbert

Cascade Books
An Imprint of Wipf and Stock Publishers
199 W. 8th Ave., Suite 3
Eugene, OR 97401

www.wipfandstock.com

PAPERBACK ISBN: 979-8-3852-6252-6
HARDCOVER ISBN: 979-8-3852-6253-3
EBOOK ISBN: 979-8-3852-6254-0

Cataloguing-in-Publication data:

Names: McDonald, Suzanne [author].

Title: Love bade me welcome : drawing nearer to God with the poems of George Herbert / Suzanne McDonald.

Description: Eugene, OR: Cascade Books, 2026 | Includes bibliographical references.

Identifiers: ISBN 979-8-3852-6252-6 (paperback) | ISBN 979-8-3852-6253-3 (hardcover) | ISBN 979-8-3852-6254-0 (ebook)

Subjects: LCSH: Herbert, George, 1593–1633. | Herbert, George, 1593–1633—Criticism and interpretation. | Devotional literature, English. | English poetry—17th century. | Christian poetry, English. | Spiritual life—Christianity. | Devotional calendars.

Classification: PR3508 M33 2026 (print) | PR3508 (ebook)

Copyright Notifications

A version of my reflections on Herbert's poems, "Sunday" and "Denial," appeared in "George Herbert, The Psalms, and Sabbath," in James Hart Brumm, ed., *Like a Watered Garden: Essays in Honor of Carol Bechtel.* I am grateful to Reformed Church Press for permission to reproduce some of that material here.

The author and publisher also thankfully acknowledge permission to reproduce the following:

Extracts from the Book of Common Prayer, the rights in which are vested in the Crown, are reproduced by permission of the Crown's patentee, Cambridge University Press.

Prayers from the *Book of Common Order* are © 1994 by Panel on Worship of the Church of Scotland. Published by St Andrew Press. Used by permission. permissions@hymns-am.co.uk

Prayers from Holy Communion Order One are © 2005 by Archbishops' Council. Published by Church House Publishing. Used by permission. permissions@hymnsam.co.uk

An Easter Sunday prayer by Rev. Dr. David Gambrell, for the Office of Theology and Worship of the Presbyterian Church (U.S.A.). Used with permission.

Excerpt from *The Book of Alternative Services*, p. 346. © 1985 by The General Synod of the Anglican Church of Canada. Used with permission.

Excerpts from the Litany of Trust written by the Sisters of Life. Used with permission.

An extract from "A Prayer for Sabbath," Christ Church London. Used with permission. https://christchurchlondon.org

Extract from "A Better World," in *Heaven and Charing Cross*. © 1996 by Edmund Banyard. Used with permission.

Excerpts from *Every Moment Holy*, volume 1, © 2017 by Douglas Kaine McKelvey. Used with permission. www.EveryMomentHoly.com

Extract from *Holy Communion: Three Orders of Service* © 1980 by National Assembly of the Uniting Church in Australia. Used with permission,

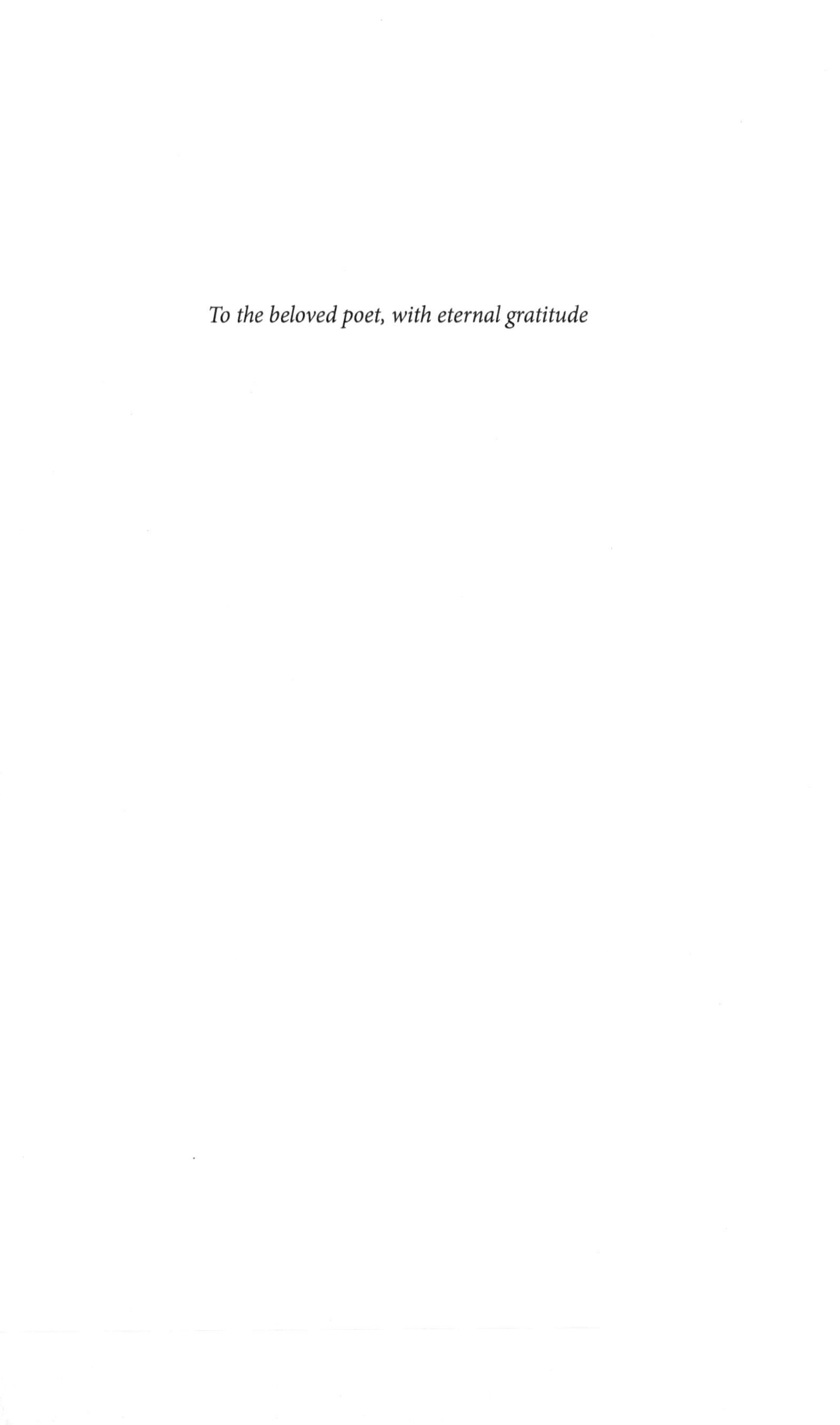

To the beloved poet, with eternal gratitude

Contents

Acknowledgments xi

Introduction xiii

The Altar 1
The Agony 5
Redemption 9
The Sepulchre 13
Easter 17
Nature 22
Sin (I) 26
Prayer (I) 30
The Holy Communion 34
Antiphon (I) 40
The Temper (I) 44
Employment (I) 49
The Quiddity 53
The Holy Scriptures (II) 57
Mattens 60
Evensong 64
The Church-Floor 69
The Windows 73
Trinity Sunday 77
Affliction (III) 81
Sunday 85
Denial 90
Christmas (Part 1) 94

The Pearl (Matthew 13) 98
Unkindness 104
Life 108
Submission 112
Justice (I) 116
Prayer (II) 120
Conscience 124
The Dawning 128
Dialogue 132
Sin's Round 136
Gratefulness 140
The Storm 145
Artillery 148
The Holdfast 153
The Collar 157
Assurance 162
The Call 167
Clasping of Hands 171
The Flower 175
A True Hymn 180
Bitter-Sweet 184
The Glance 187
Aaron 191
The Elixir 195
Death 199
Dooms-Day 203
Judgement 208
Heaven 212
Love (III) 216

Bibliography 221

Acknowledgments

WRITING THIS BOOK HAS been a deeply personal labor of love, but it has been very far from a solo enterprise. There are so many people whose insights and encouragement have carried me through, and have made this something far better than I could possibly have put together on my own.

First and foremost, I thank my parents. They were the first to read every single word. Their enthusiasm was unfailing, and their suggestions were always wise and helpful. Next, I am incredibly grateful for my wonderful reading group, who gave superbly insightful feedback on my drafts. They are congregation members, Herbert scholars, a worship minister, and a retired pastor. Between them they have helped me to keep things real, pointed out where I needed to give more (or less!) explanation, and saved me from egregious blunders in my interpretation of Herbert. David Deters, Chad Engbers, Jessica Mix, Debra Rienstra, Deb and Jim Van Schepen, I cannot thank you enough for your dedication and insight. This book is immeasurably better in every way because of your input.

Many other friends have seen some of my drafts and given me much encouragement along the way. Particular thanks go to Jeremy Begbie, Chuck DeGroat, Jim Gordon, Wesley Hill, and Walter Taylor.

It was an especial joy to share a version of some of this material with my colleague Carol Bechtel's Christianity and Literature class, and to include some reflections drawn from a draft of this book in my chapter for Carol's Festschrift.

I am also deeply grateful to the Western Theological Seminary community, who have surrounded me with so much support and encouragement in my calling as a theology professor and throughout this project. In particular, I am immensely grateful for the yearlong sabbatical I was able to take in 2023–24. This book is one of the fruits to have come from the gift of that time.

Finally, my thanks go to David Bratt and Laura Bardolph of BBH Literary without whose encouragement and help this would never have reached publication, and to my splendid editor, Robin Parry, and the team at Cascade Books.

Introduction

THE BELOVED POET

ALL OF US NEED guides and mentors in our walk with God—people who will come alongside us with loving wisdom and shrewd insight to help us to grow toward maturity in Christ. Ideally, they are people who have travelled further down the road of faith and discipleship than we have, and who have been through a good deal in their lives and in their relationship with God. We want them to be people who love the Lord, are saturated in Scripture, and who see deeply into the human heart. We also need them to be honest with us. We look to them not only to encourage us, but also to be able to tell us some home truths.

This book is an invitation to spend time with just such a person: the seventeenth-century poet and pastor George Herbert. By the Spirit, his poetry has continued to draw people to Christ, and to lead them into a deeper relationship with the triune God, a more honest faith, and a more robust discipleship, for nearly four hundred years.

I am one of the countless thousands who thank God for him. I owe more to Herbert than to almost anyone else. By God's grace, he led me to faith when I first encountered his poetry in my late teens. That was over thirty years ago, and he has been a beloved guide and mentor to me in my faith, discipleship, and calling ever since. My academic writing on his poetry set me on a course that led me from Australia to the UK, and from English literature to theology. His poetry and prose were constant companions as I wrestled with whether or not I was called to church ministry. He has continued to be a formative influence on me in what has turned out to be my primary calling as a theology professor in the United States. In my journey from unbelief to faith, over decades of seeking to grow in faith and discipleship, across academic disciplines and across continents, almost nothing about who I am and what I do would be as it is without the one who is quite simply "the beloved poet" to me.

This book is my response of love and gratitude for all that Herbert has meant to me, and it is written above all with the prayer that you will find him to be the kind of wise, gentle, witty, shrewd, loving, and generous-hearted companion on your journey that he has been on mine. If you already know Herbert and his poetry, I hope you will enjoy his company and benefit from his wisdom in a somewhat different way than you might have done before. If you don't yet know Herbert, I hope that through this book you will discover him to be for you even a fraction of what he has been for me.

But who was he? And what is it about his poetry that has had such an influence on so many people down the centuries?

INTRODUCING GEORGE HERBERT

Herbert was born in 1593, the seventh of Richard and Magdalen Herbert's ten children. His father died when he was three, and Magdalen went on to raise her family in Oxford while Herbert's oldest brother was a student there, and then in London. She remarried in 1609, and all the evidence suggests that her new husband, Sir John Danvers, was a good and kind stepfather. Herbert remained close to him and to his stepfamily for the rest of his life.

Herbert's immediate family were members of the gentry—what we might term "upper class," but not at the highest level of status and wealth. Another branch of the Herbert family, the earls of Pembroke, were among the wealthiest and most important members of the nobility. Most summers, for example, King Charles I spent weeks at a time staying at Wilton House, the Pembroke estate near Salisbury.

Herbert grew up amid a literary golden age. Shakespeare died when Herbert was twenty-three, and there were many other significant playwrights and poets at that time. His family was in the thick of the multifaceted cultural flourishing of the early seventeenth century largely because of his mother, who was a great patron of literature and the arts. Herbert was quite literally surrounded by poets, writers, and musicians, who were constant visitors to the family home. Another poet who became a priest, John

Donne, was a very frequent guest and close friend. He dedicated poems to Magdalen and preached her funeral sermon.

Herbert went to Trinity College, Cambridge, and rose up the academic ranks, becoming a fellow and then reader in rhetoric and then deputy orator of the university. His original plan had been to pursue theology and then parish ministry, but when he knew that the post of orator was about to fall vacant, he went after it and was elected in 1620. This was one of the most prestigious positions in the university. Among other duties, the orator was required to give erudite and witty speeches in Latin on behalf of the university on the hot topics of the day, and at all the major events, including when the king and his court came to Cambridge. Initially Herbert enjoyed it, and he was ambitious for where it might lead him. The oratorship was seen as a stepping-stone to a position at the royal court, an ambassadorship, or high political office.

Herbert has often been depicted as someone who rejected the glittering public career that his rank in society and his academic brilliance had set before him, and who instead chose the humble path of becoming a pastor. It wasn't *quite* like that.

As we've seen, Herbert initially felt a call to church ministry but turned aside from it, at least temporarily, to seek the oratorship. From letters we know that friends and family wondered whether that was the right thing for him to do, but it seems he was eager for the kind of future that the oratorship might open up for him.

In the end, though, that simply wasn't how things turned out. It seems that he did attract the favorable notice of King James I, but it never led to anything. The 1620s also saw the deaths of some of his prominent friends and patrons who might have helped him to gain a prestigious position. Others fell out of favor when Charles I succeeded to the throne in 1625, and still others opposed the direction the new king was taking in church matters.

By the time Herbert was in his thirties his hopes seem to have crumbled. His oldest brother, Edward, had been the English ambassador to Paris. His younger brother, Henry, already had a position at court. Herbert had the oratorship, but nothing else had come of it. He was seriously ill for much of this time and moved in with friends and family members. He left most of the work of the oratorship to his deputy and was struggling to know what to do with the rest of his life.

Without question, Herbert came to see all of this as the providence of God at work, but as some of his poems make clear, that doesn't mean he was happy about it. It also took quite some time before he felt ready to turn again to the possibility of entering the ministry. All the indications are that he held a very high view of what this calling entailed, and he was not prepared to see it merely as a pragmatic option for another "job." If he couldn't be sure that he had a genuine calling, he would not presume to take it upon himself to become a pastor.

His mother died in 1627, and he resigned the oratorship later that year after the sale of some property within the family gave him financial independence. Still unwell and unsure about his next steps, he went to live at the home of his stepfather's older brother, the earl of Danby. While he was there, he met Jane Danvers, a member of his extended stepfamily, and they married in 1629. Although they had no children of their own, they took in Herbert's three orphaned nieces. The occasional glimpses we get of their life together suggest that the marriage was a happy one and that the girls were much loved, including by Jane's extended family.[1]

In 1630 Herbert accepted the position of rector of the parish of Fugglestone-with-Bemerton just outside Salisbury. Many were astonished that someone of his background would serve in such an insignificant rural backwater, but as I've indicated, the reality for Herbert was almost certainly more complex than the myth of him nobly relinquishing worldly advancement for the life of an obscure parish priest. It seems as though he came to his calling through disappointment and struggle, even as he finally found peace and fulfillment in it for the last years of his life.

One of Herbert's curates took responsibility for St Peter's in Fugglestone, and Herbert focused his ministry on the smaller church of St Andrew's in Bemerton, where he and his family lived in the rectory across the road from the church. Herbert used to walk the mile or so into Salisbury twice a week for Evensong at the cathedral, and then he and some of the cathedral musicians would spend time singing and playing music together afterwards. About the same distance from Bemerton in the opposite direction is Wilton House, the estate of Herbert's powerful kinsman, the earl of Pembroke, where he was a frequent visitor.

1. After Herbert's death, it looks like Jane took Herbert's two surviving nieces to live with her when she returned to her father's home. It wasn't until six years after Herbert's death that she married again.

From the few hints that we have, it seems that Herbert was a caring pastor who was much loved by his parishioners, but he was able to serve them for only a few years. He died, probably of tuberculosis, on March 1, 1633, just before what would have been his fortieth birthday on April 3. The men of the Salisbury Cathedral choir came to sing at his funeral.

His parishioners would have had no idea that their pastor was also a poet. Very few people did. He may have circulated some of his poems among his family and close friends, but only a handful of his Latin poems appeared in print during his lifetime. Not long before he died, he asked a friend to deliver the manuscript of his collected poems to his dear friend Nicholas Ferrar, whom he had known since his Cambridge days. He is reported to have said:

> Sir, I pray deliver this little book to my dear brother Ferrar, and tell him he shall find in it a picture of the many spiritual conflicts that have passed betwixt God and my soul, before I could subject mine to the will of Jesus my Master, in whose service I have now found perfect freedom; desire him to read it and then if he can think it may turn to the advantage of any dejected poor soul, let it be made public; if not let him burn it, for I and it are less than the least of God's mercies.[2]

Ferrar realized what a great treasure had been entrusted to him, and *The Temple*, as this collection of Herbert's English poems is known, came out later that year. It begins with a lengthy poem called "The Church Porch," which reads rather like a series of proverbs. It ends with "The Church Militant," a long narrative poem on the history of the church. The main section in between is called "The Church" and it contains over 160 shorter poems. All of Herbert's best-known poems—and all the poems in this devotional—are from this central portion of *The Temple.*

It became an instant best seller, going through six editions by 1641 and eleven by the end of the 1600s. Down the centuries, his poetry has influenced and inspired many other poets, and a number of his poems have been set to music. Above all, though, his poems have drawn countless people into a deeper relationship with the Lord. Why?

2. This is quoted in Izaak Walton's *The Life of Mr George Herbert*, which you can find in Tobin, *George Herbert*, 310–11.

INTRODUCING GEORGE HERBERT'S POETRY

No one would still be reading Herbert if he weren't a dazzlingly gifted poet. Almost every single poem in "The Church" is in a different poetic form, for example, and as we'll see it's not just his words but also the structure of his poems, and even their layout, which all come together to draw us into the ups and downs of his life with God.

His willingness to let us into those ups and downs is one of the reasons why his poetry has continued to speak to so many of us. It's as if we are eavesdropping on Herbert's relationship with God, and that relationship was complex. Herbert has sometimes been portrayed as almost a caricature of the idea of a saint: nearly unapproachable in holiness, dauntingly pious, the "perfect" Christian and the "perfect" pastor . . . if by "perfect" we mean "without any perceptible flaws." Herbert would have been appalled by this, and it doesn't remotely reflect what we see in his poems.

As he said in his message to Ferrar, his poems are the record of his spiritual conflicts. Herbert often struggled, in himself and with God, and by letting his poems become public he has invited us into his struggles. Even though we can't always simply identify the "I" of his poems with Herbert himself, the poems are very clearly deeply personal, and the person who emerges from them is as messed up as any of the rest of us. Herbert's willingness to be honest about this—to bare his soul to God and to us—is a powerful example that helps to lead us toward greater honesty and vulnerability too.

A good number of the poems seem to track closely with events and experiences in his life, as a reminder that Herbert was a pilgrim on the way. Just like us, he was trying to work out what God was up to, and who he was in relation to God, in the midst of the messiness of life. Sometimes he's running joyfully along a smooth path, sometimes he's falling headlong into a deep and muddy ditch. That's the kind of saint he was. That's the kind of saint we can relate to, and whom we would want to have as a guide and companion on our own journey. He may not be "perfect" in the way that some have wanted to depict him, but he is perfect for us because we get to see him, identify with him, and learn from him, at his best and at his worst.

Herbert's poetry invites us to undertake the same kind of inner work that he clearly did. This means that there is a huge spiritual and emotional range in "The Church." The poems in this devotional will encompass everything from joy, gratitude, trust, praise, and a profound awareness of God's loving presence, to confusion, lament, rebellion, spiritual depression, and a sense of utter abandonment. You will find poems that resonate deeply with you, perhaps giving words to experiences you've had in your relationship with God that you might not have been able to express before. You will also find poems that challenge you and make you feel deeply uncomfortable. Herbert stretches all of us spiritually so that we can grow up into Christ.

Many of his poems are prayers. They help to cultivate a spirit of prayer in us, and they show us a variety of different ways to pray. More generally, they model for us how prayer is an intimate, honest conversation with God which also transforms us. We'll often see this in action, as Herbert moves from misunderstanding toward a better way of being, knowing, and doing, perhaps within a single poem, perhaps over a sequence of poems. It isn't simply a matter of linear progress, though. "The Church" doesn't move straightforwardly from a troubled beginning to a serene end. The poems are all over the place, all the way through. That is true to Herbert's experience of life with God, and ours as well. As we know, life in Christ often looks more like one step forward, two steps back.

Even so, Herbert does give us a sense of growing maturity along the way, and always, always, there is love. Love is the heartbeat of Herbert's poetry. Even in the midst of his struggles and rebellion we see that he is held in the unbreakable love of God. Behind all the hurt and confusion he sometimes feels, we see his longing for God and his love for God. In our journey with Herbert, he will make sure that we always know that we are loved by God, and he will lead us to love God more deeply.

Something else about Herbert's poetry is that almost from the outset it has been cherished by people on opposite sides of very deep divisions. Starting within a decade of his death, what we know today as Britain was torn apart by wars fueled by major religious and political differences. Herbert's poetry was beloved by people on all sides. This aspect of how his poetry has been received has continued down the centuries. People of all denominations and none—people who wouldn't or couldn't worship in each other's churches—have found common ground in discovering George Herbert as a guide and mentor. His poetry has been able to unite people across deep divides because most of the time he points us to aspects of faith and discipleship that all of us can share, rather than to issues that drive us apart. May this continue to be true in our own time.

You now have a sense of how a poet who died before he turned forty nearly four hundred years ago, who never made a huge mark in the world during his life, and who spent the last few years of his life as the pastor of a small rural church, has become a treasured companion in Christ to so many. Next there is a brief guide to what to expect from this book, and then we'll begin our journey with George Herbert!

A ROAD MAP FOR OUR JOURNEY

There are devotionals on fifty-two of Herbert's poems in this book so that, if you wish, you can sit with one poem per week over the course of a year. Whether or not you decide to do that, the structure of the devotionals is designed to help you to slow down and take time, not just over the poems, but also as you make connections between the poems and your life, and as you reflect with God on your walk with him.

Here's what to expect:

Poem: After a few introductory sentences you will find the text of the poem. Footnotes provide explanations for words and phrases that might be unfamiliar to you. You might prefer to simply read the poem through first, though, without being distracted by the notes, and then to check the explanations afterwards.

Reflect: This section is intended to draw out some themes and offer some guidance for interpreting the poem, with the aim of helping you to make connections between the poem and your life.

Scripture: I suggest a Scripture text for you to hold in conversation with the poem. The Holy Spirit might well prompt you to turn to other Scripture passages as well!

Dwell: Here you'll find five prompts to guide your ongoing reflections. The first two are always the same, and the final three are tailored to the specifics of each poem. You can sit with each of these points in turn, or you might prefer to focus on just one or two that particularly connect with you. These points could also spark another train of thought entirely—go wherever the Holy Spirit leads you!

Pray: I offer a prayer that reflects some of the themes of the poem. The prayers come from a variety of sources, historic and contemporary. You might want to pray these prayers, or they might become a starting point for your own.

Going Forward: Each devotional closes by asking you to notice and give thanks for the work that God has been doing in you through the poem, and to be attentive to any next steps God might be prompting you to take.

You might like to journal your way through the devotionals. That's how all of this started for me. During Covid I decided to read through all of Herbert's poetry and prose as a spiritual practice. So much bubbled up in me—about what Herbert wrote, and about my life, faith, and discipleship—that I decided to journal as I went along. In many ways, this book is the fruit of that process.

Just as you will never exhaust a Herbert poem in one reading, my hope is that this book won't simply be "one and done" for you. I hope that you will return to it many times, and find the Holy Spirit nudging you toward different insights and connections each time.

Especially for those of you who already know and love Herbert's poetry, my apologies if your favorite poem isn't in here! With just a few exceptions, I have mostly chosen some of his shorter poems, and I also wanted to share poems that represent the variety of tone and style that we find in "The Church." My selection follows the order of *The Temple* with one exception. I have placed "The Quiddity" earlier than Herbert does, to pick up on a theme from the poem that precedes it in this book ("Employment I").

The layout of his poems mattered greatly to Herbert. I have followed the first printed edition as closely as possible. For those of you who have your own preferred edition of his poetry, you might notice some differences in spelling and punctuation. I have made my own decisions on modernizing spelling (or not) and have sometimes quietly made changes to the original punctuation where I think this might help contemporary readers to follow Herbert's train of thought more easily.

One thing to note along these lines is that for words ending in "ed" I have put ~èd when these would have been pronounced with an extra syllable in Herbert's time, and I have kept his old-fashioned ~'d when the extra syllable isn't needed. So, for example, if you see "returnèd," that means you need to hear it in your head with three syllables ("re-turn-ed"), but if you see "return'd" then it is as we would pronounce it today ("re-turned"). This will help to make sure that you "hear" Herbert's lines with the right number of syllables.

Finally, a clarification with regard to the Book of Common Prayer (BCP). Whenever I mention the BCP, I am referring to the 1662 edition as it is used in the Church of England. I will always indicate this, to avoid confusion with other prayer books of the same title in other countries. Given that Herbert died in 1633, he very evidently did not use the 1662 edition (!), but there are relatively few changes between the BCP he knew and the 1662 version which is readily available today.

GOING DEEPER

While I hope the explanatory notes to the poems are helpful, especially for those of you who might not be familiar with Herbert or seventeenth-century English, there is absolutely no way that these, and my short reflections, can do more than scratch the surface of all that Herbert is seeking to convey. I simply offer a snapshot of some aspects of each poem, with how these might connect to our lives and our faith particularly in mind. There are vastly more riches to be found in his poems than I have been able to hint at here! If reading this devotional whets your appetite to go deeper into Herbert's life and writing, here are some suggestions:

The Penguin Classics edition of Herbert's works—*George Herbert: The Complete English Poems*, edited by John Tobin—is readily available and has helpful interpretive notes. It also contains poems that Herbert didn't include in the manuscript of *The Temple*, his prose work *The Country Parson*, and Izaak Walton's 1670 biography of Herbert.

If you want to explore the poems in much greater depth, you could turn to *The English Poems of George Herbert*, edited by Helen Wilcox for Cambridge University Press. In addition, Oxford University Press is in the process of publishing a three-volume edition of Herbert's complete works. This will become the standard academic edition.

If you would like to learn more about Herbert's life, with an exploration of some of his poems woven in, I recommend John Drury's *Music at Midnight: The Life and Poetry of George Herbert.*

And now as we turn to his poems, by the Holy Spirit may George Herbert be a blessing to you, as he has been to me!

The Altar

This is the first poem in "The Church," which is the main collection of poems in *The Temple*, and it is our entryway into Herbert's poetry too. Our initial reaction might be to admire it as a clever pattern poem—it's in the shape of an altar—and also to appreciate the simplicity of Herbert's language. As always with his poems, though, there's more going on than we might notice at first. Here, Herbert knows that the way to heal our broken hearts, and to soften our stony hearts, is to hold us within the story of God's redeeming love.

A broken ALTAR, Lord, thy servant rears,
Made of a heart and cemented with tears:
Whose parts are as thy hand did frame;
No workman's tool hath touch'd the same.
A HEART alone
Is such a stone,
As nothing but
Thy pow'r doth cut.
Wherefore each part
Of my hard heart
Meets in this frame,
To praise thy name:
That if I chance to hold my peace,[1]
These stones to praise thee may not cease.
O let thy blessèd SACRIFICE be mine,
And sanctify this ALTAR to be thine.

1. "To hold my peace" means to stay silent.

REFLECT

A broken ALTAR, Lord, thy servant rears

I suspect that many of us know what it is like to have a broken heart. What does the image of a stony heart mean to you? Resistance to God and God's ways? A lack of kindness and compassion? Something else?

Through the *words* of this poem, Herbert invites us to take our broken, stony hearts to the cross. And yet . . . do you notice that the altar *isn't* broken? The poem is a perfect altar shape. In the *shape* of the poem, Herbert is showing us that even as we pray, our prayer has been heard. Christ has lovingly re-shaped us and put our pieces back together.

Another way that this poem helps to put our broken pieces back together is to show us how our stories belong within the story of Scripture. Like many of Herbert's poems, this one is saturated in biblical allusions that we could easily miss. Once we notice them, we realize that Herbert is placing himself—and us—within the whole story of God's creating and redeeming love.

He reminds us that God is the one who has created/framed us. He draws us into confession and repentance as we acknowledge our broken and stony hearts and long for God to make us whole. Psalm 51:17 could be the framing verse for the poem: "The sacrifice of God is a troubled spirit: a broken and contrite heart, O God, shalt thou not despise" (1662 BCP, which is the version Herbert probably knew best).

And then, did you find yourself wondering what the third and fourth lines were about? In Exodus 20:25 and Deuteronomy 27:1–8 God tells the people of Israel they must make altars only with uncut stones. It's as if God is saying, "I don't want anything clever or fancy. Just use the simple things I've provided for you."

Between these texts and the image of a stony, broken heart as an altar, Herbert gives us a summary of the whole story of God's covenant love. Exodus 20:25 comes right after the giving of the Ten Commandments, written on tablets of stone. The Deuteronomy passage comes just before Israel enters the promised land, when they are to write the commandments on the uncut stones of the altar. We know, though, that in the new covenant, the Lord will write his law not on *stones*, but on people's *hearts* (Jeremiah 31:33).

And then toward the end Herbert brings us to the fulfillment of the new covenant in Christ. We find ourselves with the crowds on Palm Sunday, as the Pharisees demand that Jesus rebuke his disciples for shouting their praises. Jesus answers them, "I tell you that if these should hold their peace, the stones would immediately cry out" (Luke 19:40 KJV). Finally, we join Herbert at the cross as he prays: "Let thy blessed sacrifice be mine, and sanctify this altar to be thine."

As simple as this poem seems, once we pick up on the scriptural allusions, we see that in just a few lines Herbert has told the whole story of God's relationship with his people. More than that, he shows us that we and our stories belong within God's story. In response, we join Herbert in asking that the altar of our hearts and lives might be sanctified by all that Christ has done for us, so that we can become like a letter from Christ, written by the Holy Spirit on our hearts (2 Corinthians 3:3).

SCRIPTURE: PSALM 51:10–17

DWELL

- Which words, images, or phrases from the poem stand out to you? Ask the Holy Spirit to speak to you through them.
- What thoughts, feelings, or actions are prompted in you as you bring the poem and the Scripture text into conversation with each other? Hold these promptings before God.
- Do you feel—or have you ever felt—as though your heart has been broken in pieces and held together with tears? Take your broken heart to the Lord who holds all your tears (Psalm 56:8), asking him to shape and mend it.
- Reflect on how your heart might be hard and stony. Pray that the Holy Spirit might turn it into an altar of praise and thanksgiving, so that your life might become a holy and living sacrifice (Romans 12:1; Hebrews 13:15–16).
- One image (a broken heart as an altar) and one verse (Psalm 51:17) lie behind this extraordinarily dense poem. Spend some time dwelling with one of your favorite Scripture verses or images. (If it is an image, you might like to draw it, as Herbert "drew" an altar with this poem.) Be alert to what the Holy Spirit might show you about yourself through it. What connections might the Holy Spirit lead you to make

between this image/verse and the rest of the Scripture, and between your story and the scriptural story?

PRAY

O thou who camest from above,
the pure celestial fire to impart,
kindle a flame of sacred love
on the mean altar of my heart . . .

Jesus, confirm my heart's desire
to work and speak and think for thee.
Still let me guard the holy fire
and still stir up thy gift in me.[2]

GOING FORWARD

Notice—and give thanks for—the work that God has been doing in you through this poem. Be attentive to any next steps God might be inviting you to take.

2. This is an extract from one of Charles Wesley's greatest hymns. If you know it, you might like to sing the whole hymn as your prayer: https://hymnary.org/text/o_thou_who_camest_from_above.

The Agony

Herbert was no anti-intellectual. As we saw in the introduction to his life, he was a fellow at Trinity College, Cambridge, before rising to the lofty position of university orator. But in this poem, he says that there are just two things all of us ought to know about, and they don't require us to undertake vast research or pile up academic degrees. They require us only to look to Jesus.

  Philosophers have measur'd mountains,[1]
Fathom'd the depths of seas, of states, and kings,
Walk'd with a staff to heav'n, and tracèd fountains:
  But there are two vast, spacious things,
The which to measure it doth more behove:[2]
Yet few there are that sound them; Sin and Love.

  Who would know Sin, let him repair
Unto Mount Olivet; there shall he see
A man so wrung with pains, that all his hair,
  His skin, his garments bloody be[3]
Sin is that press and vice,[4] which forceth pain
To hunt his cruel food through ev'ry vein.

1. In Herbert's time, the term "philosopher" was used for experts in any academic field, hence the wide-ranging kinds of knowledge in these lines, from what we would call geology and biology to politics and astronomy.

2. This line means: that it would be more fitting to measure.

3. The agony in the garden of Gethsemane, as recounted in Luke 22:39–46.

4. The image here is of a winepress; the "vice" is the mechanism that compresses the grapes.

Who knows not Love, let him assay,[5]
And taste that juice, which on the cross a pike
Did set again abroach;[6] then let him say
If ever he did taste the like.
Love is that liquor sweet and most divine,
Which my God feels as blood; but I, as wine.

REFLECT

Love is that liquor sweet and most divine,
Which my God feels as blood; but I, as wine.

Do you sometimes feel overwhelmed by all the things you don't know? The information overload available online can leave us feeling completely inadequate. But then, those of us who have studied something deeply can fall into the trap of basing our sense of worth on what we know, presuming that because we are more knowledgeable than some people about some things, we are superior to them in everything.

As Herbert makes clear here, we might acquire a vast array of knowledge on many topics, but all of that is irrelevant compared to the most important things we need to know: the depths of sin, and the even greater depths of God's love. And this knowledge is readily available to everyone.

To see the true hideousness of sin, Herbert invites us to "Go to Dark Gethsemane" as the old hymn puts it. This stanza shows us that it was not simply the prospect of crucifixion that horrified Jesus. It was dying *for sin* that made him plead with the Father and caused him to sweat blood. Herbert draws on the traditional image of a winepress here. It has a rich scriptural history, associated with both the joy of wine and the judgment of God. It is more often linked to the cross itself, and Herbert will suggest that connection, too, at the end. But here, he uses it to convey the visceral agony that Jesus endured in the garden as he anticipated taking upon himself the full weight and consequences of sin. We can begin to know the magnitude of sin only by recognizing that the sinless one was made sin for us, so that in him we might become the righteousness of God (2 Corinthians 5:21).

5. "Assay" means try.

6. See John 19:31–37, where the soldier pierces Christ's side, causing blood and water to flow from his body (setting it abroach, to use Herbert's language here).

And then, how do we know love? As Romans 5:8 tells us, we know the love of God for us in that while we were still sinners Christ died for us. But Herbert reminds us that we do not simply know the love of God by thinking about it. We can know the love of God in the very depths of our being by *tasting* it at the communion table. Here we receive the cup of salvation (Psalm 116:13) and taste and see that the Lord is indeed good (Psalm 34:8). In this final stanza, Herbert is drawing on a traditional link between the blood that flows from Christ's pierced side and the wine/juice we receive at communion. From the crushing winepress of the weight of our sin comes the sweet wine of our salvation.

SCRIPTURE: JOHN 19:28–37

DWELL

- Which words, images, or phrases from the poem stand out to you? Ask the Holy Spirit to speak to you through them.
- What thoughts, feelings, or actions are prompted in you as you bring the poem and the Scripture text into conversation with each other? Hold these promptings before God.
- Herbert says that we rarely take the time to sound the depths of sin and love. This poem gives us his reflections on them. What are yours? Take time to ponder what those two words mean to you, and for your understanding of God. Share your thoughts with Christ in prayer.
- The Scripture text I suggested is the one Herbert draws on for the final stanza. Consider also spending time with Luke 22:39–46 or one of the other accounts of the agony in the garden (Matthew 26:36–46 or Mark 14:32–42) as you continue to reflect on the poem.
- How might it change the way you think about and experience the Lord's Supper if you focus upon it as a taste of the deep, deep love of Jesus for you?

PRAY

Almighty God,
you loved the world so much
that you sent your Son

not to condemn the world
but that through him the world might be saved.

We who are quicker to judge than to bless
fall silent at the extravagance of your grace.

As we are confronted again
with the depth of human wickedness
and the greater depth
of your divine compassion,
may we not remain unmoved.
As Christ's arms are stretched out
and his body lifted up,
may we confess our part in the sin of the world,
repent of it,
know the reality of your forgiveness,
and be transformed.
Amen.[7]

GOING FORWARD

Notice—and give thanks for—the work that God has been doing in you through this poem. Be attentive to any next steps God might be inviting you to take.

7. This is a prayer for Holy Week from the Church of Scotland's *Book of Common Order*, 438.

Redemption

This story-poem confronts us afresh with our need for the gospel, our attempts to construct an image of Jesus that fits more comfortably with our expectations, and the magnitude of what the Son of God has done for us. As you'll see, Herbert is also a master of mic-drop final lines.

Having been tenant long to a rich Lord,
        Not thriving, I resolvèd to be bold,
        And make a suit[1] unto him, to afford
A new small-rented lease, and cancel th'old.[2]

In heaven at his manor I him sought;
        They told me there that he was lately gone
        About some land, which he had dearly bought
Long since on earth, to take possession.

I straight[3] return'd, and knowing his great birth,[4]
        Sought him accordingly in great resorts;[5]

1. "Suit" means formal request. Hebrews 4:16 reminds us that in Christ we can boldly approach the throne of grace in expectation of a merciful hearing.

2. The old and new leases represent the Jewish law (the old covenant) and the gospel (the new covenant). Texts like Colossians 2:13–15 and Galatians 3:10–14 provide the background for Herbert's nexus of ideas here: how the legal debt of the law has been cancelled by the cross of Christ, how we cannot be set right with God through the works of the law, and how Christ took on the penalties of the law for us on the cross, setting our relationship with God on a new footing.

3. "Straight" here and in the final line means straight away, immediately.

4. "Great birth" means noble lineage: this is the Son of God. But Herbert is also expecting us to pick up an ironic reference to the actual birth of Jesus, which was as lowly as it could possibly be.

5. "Great resorts" means eminent locations.

In cities, theatres, gardens, parks, and courts.
At length I heard a ragged noise and mirth

Of thieves and murderers; there I him espied,
Who straight, *Your suit is granted*, said, and died.

REFLECT

At length I heard a ragged noise and mirth
Of thieves and murderers; there I him espied

Where do you expect to encounter Jesus? Where have you looked for him, and where have you actually found him?

We know from Scripture that Jesus is very often found among the least and the lost, and those who offend the "religious" people or make them feel uncomfortable. That's not where the tenant in this poem expects to find him, and it's very often not where we look for him either.

Before we get to that question, though, Herbert has another for us: What is the foundation of your relationship with God?

For that we need to spend some time with the first stanza. Just as Jesus often depicts aspects of daily life in his parables, Herbert opens this poem with a common situation for many in seventeenth-century England: a struggling tenant farmer who would like to negotiate a lower rent with the lord of the manor. It doesn't take much to update this for our own time. I suspect that many of us know what it is like to want to obtain more favorable terms for our rent, our leases, or our loans.

The tenant knows he has a rich and gracious Lord who will hear his request. As he discovers, though, while the new lease will be very favorable for him, it comes at an incalculable cost for his Lord, who, although he was rich, became poor so that we might become rich (2 Corinthians 8:9).

Behind the tenant's desire for a new lease is the contrast between living under the law (the old lease under which the tenant is not thriving) and under the gospel, in which we are set right with God through what Christ has done, by grace through faith (the new lease with the lower rent).

We know with our heads that we already live in the grace of the new covenant, but if we're honest we often live as if our relationship with God were founded not on what *Christ* has done but on what *we* do.[6] Perhaps

6. Biblical scholarship helps us to take a much more nuanced view of the nature of Israel's relationship with God under Torah (the Jewish law), but behind this poem is the

we need to seek the Lord, too, not to ask for a new lease but so that he can remind us again of the terms of our new lease on life in him.

The rest of the poem is about the tenant's quest to find his Lord. He is looking in all the wrong places, led astray by where he thinks the Son of God ought to be. If he is not in heaven, then he will surely be in places of power, prestige, wealth, and leisure on earth?

And so we come back to our first question. Where do *you* expect to find Jesus? The tenant shows us what happens when we allow our expectations and preferences to direct our steps, rather than what Jesus has shown us about himself in Scripture.

When the tenant finally stumbles upon Jesus, it still has the power to shock us. Look again at the final three lines. See how the jagged line break and the physical gap before the last two lines confront us with the brutal reality of where the tenant finally finds his Lord: nailed to a cross. The "ragged noise and mirth" the tenant hears is Christ being mocked by the murderous crowd and taunted by one of the two criminals crucified with him (Luke 23:32–46).

I think we sometimes try to shield ourselves from the sheer horror of the cross by focusing so much on theological theories about it. Theological reflection *is* important, but the climax of this poem isn't thinking about a theory. It is beholding the person of Christ mocked, reviled, and dying on the cross.

And then there is the final line. God's grace always goes ahead of us. He knows what you need before you ask, and before you even know how to ask. Before the tenant can recover from his shock, and before he can even articulate his request, he has his answer:

[Christ] Your suit is granted, said, and died.

SCRIPTURE: PHILIPPIANS 2:5–11

DWELL

- Which words, images, or phrases from the poem stand out to you? Ask the Holy Spirit to speak to you through them.

---

commonplace assumption in Herbert's day that the contrast was between "faith" (the new covenant) and "works" (the old covenant).

- What thoughts, feelings, or actions are prompted in you as you bring the poem and the Scripture text into conversation with each other? Hold these promptings before God.
- We know that our relationship with God is grounded in the costly gift of redemption in Christ, and yet we often live as if we still need to secure God's love by what we do. Reflect on the ways that this can be true of you and ask God to remind you again of the grace of the gospel.
- Think back over the past week or so. Have you noticed—or missed—the presence of Jesus in what you might think of as unlikely places? Allow this poem to challenge you to look for the presence and work of Jesus in places and people you might not expect, and that might make you feel uncomfortable.
- Imagine yourself standing with the tenant in the crowd at the crucifixion. Share your thoughts and feelings with Christ in prayer.

PRAY

Thank you, Lord Jesus, for your inexpressible love.
You came from eternal blessedness and the Father's throne
into the midst of indifference, hatred, scorn, shame, and suffering
to bestow the gift of salvation.
My dearest Friend, you saw my need and gave your life to meet it.
Words will never be adequate to express what you have done,
but all my life I will offer you my thanks and praise and love.
Amen.[7]

GOING FORWARD

Notice—and give thanks for—the work that God has been doing in you through this poem. Be attentive to any next steps God might be inviting you to take.

7. I wrote this prayer based on Samuel Crossman's hymn "My Song Is Love Unknown": https://hymnary.org/text/my_song_is_love_unknown.

The Sepulchre

Herbert places this after our previous poem, "Redemption." Having stood at the foot of the cross, we now find ourselves at the tomb. Herbert also calls our minds back once more to our very first poem, "The Altar." This time, rather than our hearts being like a stone altar, Herbert compares them to a stone tomb. We don't come off well in that comparison.

O blessèd body! Whither art thou thrown?
No lodging for thee, but a cold hard stone?
So many hearts on earth, and yet not one
Receive thee?

Sure there is room within our hearts' good store;
For they can lodge transgressions by the score:
Thousands of toys[1] dwell there, yet out of door
They leave thee.

But that which shows them large, shows them unfit.[2]
What ever sin did this pure rock commit,
Which holds thee now? Who hath indicted it
Of murder?

1. "Toys" means trivial things.

2. The number of sins and trivialities our hearts can hold shows them to be large enough for Christ, but also not fit to hold him.

Where our hard hearts have took up stones to brain thee,[3]
And missing this, most falsely did arraign thee,
Only these stones in quiet entertain thee,
And order.[4]

And as of old, the law by heav'nly art
Was writ in stone; so thou, which also art
The letter of the word,[5] find'st no fit heart
To hold thee.

Yet do we still persist as we began,
And so should perish,[6] but that nothing can,
Though it be cold, hard, foul, from loving man
Withold thee.

REFLECT

No lodging for thee, but a cold hard stone?

Have you wept over the death and burial of Jesus? I have. The horror of it and the magnitude of what the Son of God has done for us is overwhelming if we allow ourselves to dwell on it. There is a problem, though. Sometimes our sorrow slides into sentimentality. We feel sad for what happened to Jesus but have no qualms about continuing to dishonor him with our lives.

Herbert ruthlessly exposes our hypocrisy. For all that we might lament at Christ's tomb, we kill and bury him afresh. We might profess Jesus as Lord, but if we're honest with ourselves, in our daily lives we are often functionally indifferent to him, and some of the things we say and do are very much contrary to Jesus and his ways.

Herbert does this by comparing the stone tomb (generously given by Joseph of Arimathea [Matthew 27:57–61]) with our ungenerous, cold,

3. "To brain thee" means to stone thee, e.g., John 8:59.

4. The pure stones of the tomb are a fit and well-ordered place to hold the body of Christ, in contrast to the sinful clutter, violence, and disorder of our stony hearts.

5. In the incarnation, Christ is the eternal Word of God "spelled out" to us, so to speak, as a "letter" we can understand.

6. Herbert is thinking here of how, ever since Adam and Eve, we have turned aside from God, with death as the penalty for sin.

stony hearts. Herbert points us back to Jesus' birth too, to show us that it has always been like this, and *we* have always been like this. Hearts that will not receive Jesus point to how the Word came to his own, but his own would not receive him (John 1:11). Our hearts being full of all sorts of sins and trivialities so that Jesus is left out of doors points us to how there was no room for Mary and Joseph (Luke 2:7).

Our stony hearts are worse than unwelcoming, though. They are downright hostile. The tomb did nothing to hurt Jesus. Its quiet stones welcomed him and gave him rest as best they could. But our sins mean that we are identified with those who picked up stones to kill him (John 8:59; 10:31–33) and with those who brought him to the cross.

Herbert's depiction of us is relentlessly, realistically bleak. It would seem that all is lost, and we are lost. But at the last moment, Herbert shifts the perspective of the poem. Thanks be to God, our reconciled relationship with God does not depend on us. At the close, Herbert reminds us of Paul's glorious words in Romans 8:31–39: that nothing can separate us from the love of God in Christ, not even our cold, hard, foul hearts.

SCRIPTURE: ROMANS 5:6–11

DWELL

- Which words, images, or phrases from the poem stand out to you? Ask the Holy Spirit to speak to you through them.
- What thoughts, feelings, or actions are prompted in you as you bring the poem and the Scripture text into conversation with each other? Hold these promptings before God.
- Ask the Holy Spirit to help you to make an inventory of the contents of your heart. What is filling it up so much that there is no room for Jesus? What clutter, and what harmful things, do you need to discard?
- Holding fast to the truth that you are loved by Jesus, dare to be honest with him about times that you have taken up stones to stone him. In what ways have your words and actions sometimes betrayed Jesus and your commitment to walk in his ways? Do this knowing that if we confess our sins, he is faithful and just to forgive us and to cleanse us (1 John 1:9).
- Up until the last few lines this whole poem is a bleak indictment of us that seems to leave us in a hopeless situation. Those last few lines

change everything. How does knowing that there is nothing about you that can make Christ withhold his love from you change everything for you?

PRAY

Loving Lord Jesus, when you came among us
those who should have welcomed you
did not receive you.
In life you had no home of your own,
and in death you lay in a stranger's tomb.
I am sorry for the ways I still do not welcome you.
Make my heart and my life more hospitable to you,
That by your love to me I might be made loving,
And so live to love and serve you.
In your name I pray.
Amen.[7]

In addition to this prayer, you might like to listen to the close of Bach's *St Matthew Passion* and/or his *St John Passion*. Both finish at the tomb. For the *St Matthew Passion*, listen from the recitative "Nun ist der Herr zur Ruh gebracht" (Now the Lord is laid to rest) to the end. For the *St John Passion*, listen to the final chorus and chorale, "Ruht wohl . . . Ach Herr" (Rest in peace . . . Ah Lord).

GOING FORWARD

Notice—and give thanks for—the work that God has been doing in you through this poem. Be attentive to any next steps God might be inviting you to take.

7. I wrote this prayer based on Samuel Crossman's hymn "My Song Is Love Unknown": https://hymnary.org/text/my_song_is_love_unknown.

Easter

In our poems so far, we have journeyed with Herbert from Palm Sunday to the garden of Gethsemane, the cross, and the tomb. Now we rejoice with him in the resurrection. The first part of this poem describes how Herbert turns to music to praise the risen Lord. The second part is a song. Herbert was a gifted musician and singer and set some of his poems to music. In all likelihood this is one of them, although sadly none of his music survives.

Rise heart; thy Lord is risen. Sing his praise
Without delays,
Who takes thee by the hand, that thou likewise
With him mayst rise:
That, as his death calcinèd thee to dust,
His life may make thee gold, and much more, just.[1]

Awake, my lute, and struggle for thy part
With all thy art.
The cross taught all wood to resound his name,
Who bore the same.
His stretchèd sinews taught all strings what key
Is best to celebrate this most high day.[2]

1. "Calcined to dust" means burned to ashes. "Just" is short for "justified" or set right with God. See more in the "Reflect" section for how Herbert is drawing on alchemy here.

2. The metaphor of the cross as a musical instrument (here, a lute) with Christ crucified as the strings which need to be stretched and tightened to tune them might seem grotesque to us, but it was common in Herbert's time. In addition, Herbert is referring to how in his time church music was set to a higher pitch than other music, requiring the strings to be tightened even further.

Consort both heart and lute, and twist a song
Pleasant and long:
Or, since all music is but three parts vied
And multiplied,
O let thy blessèd Spirit bear a part,
And make up our defects with his sweet art.[3]

I got me flowers to straw thy way;[4]
I got me boughs off many a tree:
But thou wast up by break of day,
And brought'st thy sweets along with thee.

The Sun arising in the East
Though he give light, & th'East perfume,[5]
If they should offer to contest
With thy arising, they presume.

Can there be any day but this,
Though many suns to shine endeavour?
We count three hundred but we miss:
There is but one, and that one ever.

REFLECT

Rise heart; thy Lord is risen.

We know that Jesus died for our sins and was raised for our justification (Romans 4:25), but if you are anything like me, those words can sometimes feel very abstract. What does it actually mean for us to be united to Christ in his death and resurrection (Romans 6:5)?

Herbert gives us a beautiful image to help us: Jesus holding our hand. This is one of Herbert's favorite ways of depicting Christ's intimate, tender

3. The foundational idea in these lines might be the triad (a three-part chord). The emphasis, though, is on how his heart, his lute, and the Holy Spirit make up the three-part polyphony (the three intertwining lines) of his Easter music.

4. "Straw" means bestrew. The poet wants to scatter flowers in front of the risen Christ.

5. In Herbert's day, the finest and most costly perfumes came from what we would now call the Middle East.

love, and we will encounter it many times. Christ takes your hand to raise you up with him, not just in the resurrection on the last day, but also from whatever is holding you back from experiencing more of his love right now.

Next Herbert draws on alchemy, which was the quest to discover "philosopher's gold"—the perfection of physical and spiritual matter, which would also be the elixir of eternal life. "Calcined" is an alchemical term that means burned. Christ's death reduces us to dust and ashes (recalling Genesis 3:19 and Ash Wednesday). The cross at once reveals us as sinners and destroys the power of sin in us. Christ's resurrection transforms our ashes into gold, and gives us something far more valuable even than that. Through Christ's resurrection we are justified (made "just"/set right with God), which leads us to eternal life.

With Herbert's help we can see that Christ dying for our sins and being raised for our justification means that whatever separates us from the fullness of Christ's love has been burned to ashes in the fire of his love, and from the ashes you are being transformed more and more into the gold of who you truly are: the beloved, treasured child of God.

This calls for songs of joy and praise! Herbert knows that his songs (and ours) will always fall short of what we feel, and the wonder of what Christ has done for us. But he also knows that the Lord delights in our efforts, and that the Holy Spirit himself will join in with us, perfecting our songs as he does our prayers.

In his song, Herbert tries to get up early enough to be ready with flowers and branches to offer them to Jesus at his rising. In Herbert's time, people would decorate the church with spring flowers and greenery before the Easter morning service. In his manual for pastors, Herbert speaks of how the church should be "strawed and stuck with boughs."[6] But as this song reminds us, Jesus is always ahead of us. Our small and simple gestures are always a response to what he has already graciously done and provided for us.

And then we have one of Herbert's favorite puns! It is the play on words between the sun and the Son. Here, the rising sun cannot presume to compare to the risen Son, and from now on, it is the risen Son, rather than the daily rising of the sun, that shows us what the true time is. Yes, says Herbert, with the sun we count off the three hundred or so days of each year, but Jesus' resurrection is the dawning of the eternal day. This is because, as well as defeating sin and death, Jesus' resurrection gives us a

6. Tobin, *George Herbert*, 221.

glimpse of the coming new creation and an anticipation of the fullness of eternal life. What might it mean for you to live in light of that, and to tell the time by the Son even more than by the sun?

SCRIPTURE: ROMANS 6:3–4

DWELL

- Which words, images, or phrases from the poem stand out to you? Ask the Holy Spirit to speak to you through them.
- What thoughts, feelings, or actions are prompted in you as you bring the poem and the Scripture text into conversation with each other? Hold these promptings before God.
- Herbert's response to the resurrection is to sing for joy, and it is the same for many of us! Choose one of your favorite Easter hymns/ songs—play it loud and/or sing it heartily as an offering of praise and thanksgiving to Christ!
- Are you weighed down by a sense of inadequacy and failure? Imagine Christ taking you by the hand to lift you up, and hear him telling you that you are not dust but gold; you are not worthless, but beloved. Share your response with him.
- Write a poem or reflection on Jesus' resurrection, and don't let any concerns about whether your words are "good enough" hold you back! Our words will always fall short, but the Holy Spirit delights to join in with us, and to "make up our defects with his sweet art."

PRAY

Living God, on the first day of the week
you brought to birth a new creation
through the glorious resurrection of Jesus Christ.
Fill us with the hope and joy of new beginnings,
so that we may share the good news
of your liberating, life-giving power with all the world;
through Christ our Savior, who is alive

and reigns with you and the Holy Spirit,
now and always. Amen.[7]

GOING FORWARD

Notice—and give thanks for—the work that God has been doing in you through this poem. Be attentive to any next steps God might be inviting you to take.

7. This prayer is by Rev. Dr. David Gambrell.

Nature

One of the most profound aspects of journeying with Herbert is his willingness to lay bare the "downs" as well as the "ups" of life with God. He is prepared to show us resistance as well as love. In this prayer-poem, Herbert expresses a desire both to flee and to return, holding all of this in unresolved tension before God and giving us permission to do likewise.

Full of rebellion, I would die,
Or fight, or travel, or deny
That thou hast ought to do with me.[1]
O tame my heart;
It is thy highest art
To captivate strongholds to thee.[2]

If thou shalt let this venom lurk,
And in suggestions fume and work,
My soul will turn to bubbles straight,
And thence by kind
Vanish into a wind,
Making thy workmanship deceit.[3]

1. "Ought" means anything.

2. The poet's heart is depicted as a castle (stronghold) with God besieging it. See 2 Corinthians 10:4 for this image in relation to spiritual warfare, but this is also a common metaphor from love poetry, in which the lover uses all his persuasive powers to win the beloved's heart.

3. His spirit of rebellion against God is like a poison ("venom") working a chemical reaction within him to produce his thoughts (the suggestions that "fume and work"). If all of this keeps up, the outcome will be to dissolve his soul into bubbles, which by nature

O smooth my rugged heart, and there
Engrave thy rev'rend law and fear;
Or make a new one, since the old
Is sapless grown,[4]
And a much fitter stone
To hide my dust, than thee to hold.

REFLECT

O tame my heart

Have there been times in your life when you have been frustrated with God, with yourself, with everyone and everything? Like Herbert here, we might well want to run away from God and his claim on our lives. And yet we still long for God. Or we wish we did.

Even as he rebels against God in this poem, Herbert prays, pleading with God to draw him back. This is not a broken relationship between the poet and God; it is a struggle *within* that relationship. There is something utterly real about that. It is what we find in many of the Psalms, which wrestle with God even as they are prayers to God. It is true to the experience of many of us as well. Beneath the desire to break free in this poem there remains a deep foundation of hope and trust. This is what enables Herbert to bring his whole rebellious, confused, longing self before God, and he gives us permission to do that too.

There is also something very real about Herbert's tactics to try to persuade God to thwart his own bad intentions. Notice how Herbert implies that it will be *God's* fault ("If *thou* shalt let this venom lurk") if he goes through with his rebellion and ends up lost. God wouldn't want that, surely . . . ?

Does that sound familiar? Faced with something we know is wrong, but which we want to do—and maybe even end up doing—we refuse to

("kind") vanish in the air, negating God's work in creating it ("making thy workmanship deceit"). In Herbert's day, "kind" and "wind" would have rhymed.

4. "Sapless" means lifeless. Herbert is drawing once again on the scriptural image of a heart made of stone rather than flesh, and is also picking up on the image of a stone tomb from "The Sepulchre." Here, his heart is a stony tomb for himself, rather than a place for Christ to dwell.

take responsibility for our choices. We try to throw the blame onto God instead. We've been doing that since the first sin (Genesis 3:12).

Even so, Herbert is also pointing toward a profound theological truth here which will come up many times in his poems, mostly as a source of deep assurance. Herbert knows that left to himself he would never be able to have faith in God or walk in God's ways. That is our nature (to pick up on the poem's title) under the influence of sin. He knows that it is only by God's work *in* us as well as *for* us that we can turn to him and return to our true nature as those made for right relationship with God.

So he pleads with God to win his heart back, and to smooth its rugged places. Perhaps this is an echo of making the rough places smooth, to prepare the way of the Lord (Isaiah 40:3–4; Luke 3:3–6). Notice how we are also back to the idea of a stony heart, that rich scriptural image upon which Herbert draws so often. Once again, we have allusions to God writing the law on stone tablets, and to God's promise to give his people new hearts of flesh instead of stone (Ezekiel 36:26). And as in "The Sepulchre" Herbert longs for his stony heart to be made a fit dwelling place for God.

This poem invites us to join Herbert in taking our whole confused, contradictory, messed-up selves to God. And it reminds us that when we are tossed to and fro by our feelings and our circumstances, we can still cast ourselves upon God, trusting in his sure hold on us, rather than our feeble grip on him.

SCRIPTURE: ROMANS 7:14–25

DWELL

- Which words, images, or phrases from the poem stand out to you? Ask the Holy Spirit to speak to you through them.
- What thoughts, feelings, or actions are prompted in you as you bring the poem and the Scripture text into conversation with each other? Hold these promptings before God.
- Have you ever felt like running away from God? Take the "rebellious" parts of yourself and your life to him, trusting in the Father's loving response to every son or daughter who has run away, or wanted to run away.
- Are there parts of your heart that feel rough and dry? Ask the Holy Spirit to smooth the rough places, and to give you a renewed sense of

life, love, and fruitfulness in your relationship with God, and in your discipleship.

- Even as he rebels against God, Herbert also knows God as the one who "tames" our hearts through love. What difference might it make in your relationship with God to think of him as the one who sets out to "captivate" and entrance your heart?

PRAY

> Almighty and most merciful Father, We have erred and strayed from thy ways like lost sheep, We have followed too much the devices and desires of our own hearts, We have offended against thy holy laws, We have left undone those things which we ought to have done, And we have done those things which we ought not to have done, And there is no health in us: But thou, O Lord, have mercy upon us miserable offenders; Spare thou them, O God, which confess their faults, Restore thou them that are penitent, According to thy promises declared unto mankind in Christ Jesu our Lord: And grant, O most merciful Father, for his sake, That we may hereafter live a godly, righteous, and sober life, To the glory of thy holy Name. Amen.[5]

GOING FORWARD

Notice—and give thanks for—the work that God has been doing in you through this poem. Be attentive to any next steps God might be inviting you to take.

5. This is the prayer of confession from Morning and Evening Prayer in the 1662 BCP. Herbert would have prayed this twice every day. There are some strong words in here. These days we rarely speak in terms of there being "no [spiritual] health in us" or of being "miserable offenders" (where "miserable" means both "unhappy" and "pitiful"). But this prayer fits the mood of our poem—it might even have been in the back of Herbert's mind—and sometimes, honesty compels us to recognize that these words are apt to describe how things are for us in our walk with God.

Sin (I)

As you start to read this poem you might find yourself wondering what the title has to do with the content. Almost the entire poem is about the many ways that God helps us to stay on the right path. But then Herbert skewers us with the last two lines . . .

Lord, with what care hast thou begirt us round![1]
    Parents first season us; then schoolmasters
    Deliver us to laws; they send us bound
To rules of reason, holy messengers,

Pulpits and Sundays, sorrow dogging sin,[2]
    Afflictions sorted,[3] anguish of all sizes,
    Fine nets and stratagems to catch us in,
Bibles laid open, millions of surprises,

Blessings beforehand,[4] ties of gratefulness,
    The sound of glory ringing in our ears,
    Without, our shame; within, our consciences,[5]
Angels and grace, eternal hopes and fears.

1. "Begirt" means to encircle or enclose. It relates to the idea of a girdle: an undergarment to help to shape and support the body.

2. "Dogging" means following closely after.

3. "Afflictions sorted" means assorted afflictions.

4. "Beforehand" means in advance.

5. Herbert is referring to external pressure ("without" means outside of us, so the shame that comes when other people find us out) and internal pressure (our conscience within us).

Yet all these fences and their whole array
One cunning bosom-sin blows quite away.[6]

REFLECT

One cunning bosom-sin

How has the Lord carefully "begirt you round" to help to keep you walking in his ways?

Every now and then Herbert gives us a "list" poem. The most famous is about prayer, and we will turn to it next. This one is about what Herbert calls the "fences"—what we might call the "guardrails"—that God puts along our lives to keep us on the right path. We can relate to many of these. Hopefully we too have had parents, teachers, and pastors who have sought to guide us well. God has also given us Scripture, and untold numbers of unexpected blessings, graces, and things for which to be grateful.

Notice, though, that Herbert doesn't just include what we might call "good" things in his list. There are difficult things too. He mentions how our sorrow for sin, being found out by others, and our troubled conscience are all means by which God brings us to our senses and guides us back to his ways. Afflictions and anguish of all kinds are included as well. Herbert is quietly reminding us that, in his providence, God can use even hard and painful experiences to draw us back to himself (Romans 8:28).

But then, after twelve lines of examples that are intended to leave us grateful to God for his care for us, everything comes crashing down. The thing that flattens the fences and brings down the guardrails is what Herbert calls our "bosom-sin." That language may sound very strange to us, but it was a standard term in the sermons and devotional books of his time, and it brilliantly captures what it describes. It is the sin that we cling to and embrace most closely. It is the sin we think about most, and that we least want to resist. We toy with it, and perhaps we even try to rationalize our way into believing that it isn't really a sin at all, or at least that God won't mind too much if we keep on giving in to it. As Herbert points out, bosom-sins are cunning.

Whatever form this bosom-sin takes, it is an idol. We desire and follow it more than we desire and follow God. It is sufficient to render all the ways that God uses to keep us from straying null and void, and having blown all the fences down, it will lead us to wander very far from God.

6. "Bosom-sin" means the sin we cling to the most.

That is a harsh place to leave us, but Herbert's care in arranging the sequence of his poems can help us here. Earlier, he placed a couple of poems about baptism to remind us of God's promises and faithfulness to us, as well as our calling to live in love toward God as a response to his grace. Ever the realist, though, straight after the baptism poems comes our previous poem, "Nature," to remind us of how we continue to resist God and God's ways. Then there is this poem, and after it comes a long, desolate poem called "Affliction I." But then, Herbert leads us to make a turn, with poems called "Repentance" and "Faith." Just as his individual poems find meaning within a sequence, so Herbert is reminding us that we need to see the individual episodes of our lives as part of the whole story of God's loving care for us.

SCRIPTURE: PSALM 119:33–40

DWELL

- Which words, images, or phrases from the poem stand out to you? Ask the Holy Spirit to speak to you through them.
- What thoughts, feelings, or actions are prompted in you as you bring the poem and the Scripture text into conversation with each other? Hold these promptings before God.
- Consider writing your own list of the ways that God has providentially cared for you, giving thanks to God for how he has kept you in his ways through both good and difficult circumstances.
- What is your "cunning bosom-sin"? Take it to Christ, our great High Priest, who was tempted like us, but did not sin, and who sympathizes with our weakness (Hebrews 4:14–16). Ask Christ to help you to understand its hold on you, and to show you something about himself and his ways that will be more attractive to you than your bosom-sin currently is.
- As you reflect on your circumstances now and think back over the course of your life, what difference does it make to see the episodes of your life as part of a whole (and as yet unfinished) journey with God?

PRAY

O Lord my God,
open my eyes that I might see,
incline my heart so that I might desire,
and order my steps that I might follow
the path of your commandments.
Hedge my way with thorns
so that I do not follow the path of sin.
Enable me to refuse what is evil
and cleave to what is good
so that I might follow the truth in love
to the glory of your name.
Amen.[7]

GOING FORWARD

Notice—and give thanks for—the work that God has been doing in you through this poem. Be attentive to any next steps God might be inviting you to take.

7. I wrote this prayer based on the "Comprecation" and the "Hedge of the Law" for Sunday morning prayers in Lancelot Andrewes's *Preces Privatae*, 44–45. Andrewes (1555–1626) was an eminent and influential preacher, scholar, and bishop. Herbert first encountered him as a schoolboy at the Westminster School, and Andrewes was a friend and mentor to Herbert for the rest of his life.

Prayer (I)

Here is the most famous of Herbert's "list" poems. Evocative words and images tumble over one another as he seeks to express something of the wonder, the struggle, the beauty, and the mystery of our conversation and communion with God in prayer, until we finally close with "something understood."

Prayer the church's banquet, angels' age,[1]
    God's breath in man returning to his birth,
    The soul in paraphrase, heart in pilgrimage,
The Christian plummet sounding heav'n and earth;[2]

Engine against th'Almighty,[3] sinner's tow'r,
    Reversèd thunder, Christ-side-piercing spear,[4]
    The six-days world transposing in an hour,
A kind of tune, which all things hear and fear;

Softness, and peace, and joy, and love, and bliss,
    Exalted manna, gladness of the best,
    Heaven in ordinary, man well dress'd,
The milky way, the bird of Paradise,[5]

1. The endless life of angels vs. the limited lifespan of our earthly lives.

2. A plummet is the weight at the end of a plumb line, used to sound the depths of water or to ensure a straight line in building.

3. "Engine" here refers to a siege engine (a weapon used when besieging a castle).

4. This is a reference to the soldier who pierced Christ's side on the cross (John 19:34).

5. In Herbert's day, the bird of paradise was the epitome of all that was mysterious and exotic. It was also thought that it had no feet, so that it never landed or perched.

Church-bells beyond the stars heard, the soul's blood,
The land of spices; something understood.

REFLECT

The soul in paraphrase, heart in pilgrimage

My thoughts instinctively go to personal, private prayer as I read this poem. I always need to remind myself that Herbert's very first image for prayer is "the *church's* banquet." And when he speaks of prayer "transposing" the six-day world in an hour, and being like church bells heard beyond the stars (heard by God in heaven), he almost certainly has the time of gathered worship on Sunday morning in mind, with the bells being rung to summon parishioners to church. Herbert valued and practiced various kinds of prayer, including private, extempore prayer, the set liturgy of the Church of England, and writing out his own prayers to share in public worship too. Perhaps he can be an example to us, especially if we tend to be rather judgmental about different kinds of prayer.

This poem is one long breathless sentence that isn't even a proper sentence! Herbert is so eager to launch into his multitude of ways to describe prayer that he doesn't include a verb. I wonder which images and phrases in this poem most capture your attention and speak to your own experiences of prayer? Any of them could be a focus for extended reflection. Malcolm Guite, Church of England priest and poet, has written an individual poem on each one.[6]

I especially love the idea of prayer as "God's breath in man returning to his birth." The default to masculine language might jar us initially, but there are riches here. We are taken back to the intimacy of God's breath of life in Genesis 2:7, and forward to the risen Lord breathing the Holy Spirit upon his disciples (John 20:22). Romans 8:26–27 reminds us that the Holy Spirit prays in and with us. Prayer is a gift of God to us, and the life breath of our relationship with God, just as Herbert refers to it later as the "blood" that keeps our soul alive.

And then there's a cluster of very striking images in the fifth and sixth lines. Prayer is like a siege weapon to break down God's apparent resistance or silence behind the castle walls, so to speak. But prayer is also a tower (a stronghold or castle) for sinners. This is a powerful image of God's

6. Guite, *After Prayer*. You can find Guite's poems on his blog: https://malcolmguite.wordpress.com/blog/.

protection in the Psalms (e.g., Psalms 61:3; 71:3; 144:2). We can flee to God in prayer, so that our communion with God becomes our refuge. And while thunder is usually a metaphor for God's voice and power, here it is the power of our voices in prayer. But since prayer is also God's work in us, it is also God's voice in us returning to him, just like the earlier image of God's breath. The last image in these very dense lines is of prayer as a "Christ-side-piercing spear." Traditionally, the blood and water that flowed from Christ's side represent the salvation won for us. Prayer becomes the channel by which the benefits of his saving work flow to us.

I also love how Herbert describes prayer in ways that are both grand and exotic and mundane and homely. Prayer is like the mysteries of outer space, and yet it is also the deeply personal intimacy of "softness, and peace, and love, and joy, and bliss." It is like the most outlandish thing a seventeenth-century person can think of—a bird of paradise—and also heaven in the midst of the ordinary. Prayer is to our daily lives as putting on clothes is to our bodies: We are not well dressed for the day until we have prayed.

Those final two words bring closure, but also open-ended wondering. What is the mysterious "something" that is understood? Is it prayer itself? Is it something that we have been praying about? These words make me think of the Ephesians text I have chosen to accompany this poem. This text is a prayer that asks, among other things, that we might come to know the love of Christ, which is really beyond knowing. We do know *something* of the extraordinary love of Christ, but its fullness is more than we can ever fully comprehend. Perhaps Herbert is suggesting something similar about prayer.

SCRIPTURE: EPHESIANS 3:14–21

DWELL

- Which words, images, or phrases from the poem stand out to you? Ask the Holy Spirit to speak to you through them.
- What thoughts, feelings, or actions are prompted in you as you bring the poem and the Scripture text into conversation with each other? Hold these promptings before God.
- Especially if you find it hard to pray, what difference might it make to think of prayer simply as talking to God about where you are at right

now (your "soul in paraphrase" and "heart in pilgrimage") or offering your daily life and concerns to him ("heaven in ordinary")?

- Choose an image or phrase that strikes you as strange. What is different about this and your approach to prayer? Might there be something about this image/phrase that could enrich your understanding of prayer?
- What is prayer for you? Consider writing your own list of images and phrases to express something of what prayer means to you.

PRAY

After so many words about prayer, spend time in silent prayer, resting in the "softness, and peace, and joy, and love, and bliss" of the presence of the triune God.

GOING FORWARD

Notice—and give thanks for—the work that God has been doing in you through this poem. Be attentive to any next steps God might be inviting you to take.

The Holy Communion

From his poetry and his prose, we know that Herbert dearly loved the Lord's Supper. Here he focuses on how in this sacrament Christ both comes to us and lifts us up to himself.

Not in rich furniture, or fine array,
Nor in a wedge of gold,
Thou, who from me wast sold,[1]
To me dost now thyself convey;
For so thou should'st without me still have been,[2]
Leaving within me sin:

But by the way of nourishment and strength
Thou creep'st into my breast,
Making thy way my rest,
And thy small quantities my length;
Which spread their forces into every part,
Meeting sin's force and art.

Yet can these not get over to my soul,
Leaping the wall that parts
Our souls and fleshly hearts;
But as th' outworks,[3] they may control

1. Some drafts of this poem have "for me" and some "from me." "From me" was the final choice to match "to me" in the next line.

2. "So thou shouldst without me still have been" means if that had been the case, you would still/always have been outside of me.

3. "Outworks" are defensive structures to protect a castle (here, our soul). The physical elements defend the outworks to help to control our "rebel flesh" but cannot reach the inner sanctum of our souls.

My rebel-flesh, and carrying thy name,
Affright both sin and shame.

Only thy grace, which with these elements comes,
Knoweth the ready way,
And hath the privy key,[4]
Op'ning the soul's most subtle rooms:
While those[5] to spirits refin'd, at door attend
Dispatches from their friend.[6]

Give me my captive soul, or take
My body also thither.[7]
Another lift like this will make
Them both to be together.

Before that sin turn'd flesh to stone,
And all our lump to leaven;
A fervent sigh might well have blown
Our innocent earth to heaven.

For sure when Adam did not know
To sin, or sin to smother;[8]
He might to heav'n from Paradise go,[9]
As from one room t' another.

---

4. "Privy" means secret.

5. "Those" signifies the physical elements of bread and wine.

6. "Attend / Dispatches from their friend" means await letters from Christ (since they cannot go through the "door" from body to soul).

7. The idea here is that in receiving communion, Christ has taken his soul captive—you might say, Christ has "captivated" his soul—such that his soul is with Christ. He is asking for his soul back, or better, for Christ to take his body too so that he can be fully with Christ.

8. These two lines describe Adam before he knew what sin was, or what it meant to resist it.

9. Paradise here signifies Eden.

Thou hast restor'd us to this ease
By this thy heav'nly blood,
Which I can go to, when I please,
And leave th' earth to their food.

REFLECT

But by the way of nourishment and strength
Thou creep'st into my breast

How do you respond to the arguments raging on social media and elsewhere? It seems like every day, and sometimes every few hours, another hot-button issue arises to wind us up, and make us feel like we ought to join the pile-on.

Herbert wrote another poem called "Holy Communion." It was learned, witty, and snarky.[10] He omitted it from his final collection. In effect, he decided not to hit "send" on his smart-aleck response to debates about the Lord's Supper, which was one of the hot-button issues of his day.

He chose to include this poem instead. Here, rather than showing us how clever he is, Herbert points us to Christ. Instead of focusing on what he is against, he tells us what he is for. Instead of mocking those he disagrees with and stoking polarization, Herbert is hospitable, emphasizing themes that can be shared across theological differences.

When it comes to engaging in debate, be like Herbert.

And then, what does the Lord's Supper mean to you? Has it meant different things to you at different times in your life? How often does your church celebrate communion? Do you use a set liturgy, or are the words more informal? Do you go forward to receive the bread and wine/juice or are the elements brought to you? How do those aspects of how your church celebrates the sacrament shape your experience of it?

We will all have very different responses to these questions, but we can all join Herbert in marveling at the humble intimacy of how Christ comes to us: not in opulent grandeur but through commonplace bits of bread and wine.

10. For example, against the view that Christ is in some way physically present in the elements he wrote: "Whether bread stay / Or whether bread do fly away / Concerneth bread not me . . . I could believe an Impanation / At the rate of an Incarnation / If thou hadst died for bread."

The elements are also a reminder that we don't come to know Christ simply through words and ideas. We also come to know him as the host at his table, offering us food and drink to nourish our bodies as well as our souls. In turn, we are called to present our bodies as a living sacrifice to God (Romans 12:1), and to live so that our whole selves are instruments of righteousness rather than sin (Romans 6:12–13).

In this poem, the sacrament helps to defend us, body and soul, from the attacks of sin. As the physical elements help to sanctify our physical bodies, so the grace that comes with the elements penetrates to the depth of our souls. The grace of the sacrament is the spiritual presence of Christ to us and in us. Not only does Christ come to us, he also lifts us up to him, echoing the ancient communion liturgy that asks us to lift up our hearts to the Lord. For Herbert, receiving communion is the closest we can get to the intimacy with God that Adam and Eve enjoyed before sin.[11]

This is because at its heart, the Lord's Supper is about our union with Christ. In an earlier poem ("Easter") we reflected on how this is a beautiful concept, but it can be hard to grasp what it actually means. The Lord's Supper helps us to experience something of it. As the elements become part of our bodies, so also, when we receive the supper in faith, we are more deeply united to Christ and he to us.

I think Herbert is right to focus our attention on themes like this. Above and beyond all the debates about this sacrament, all of us can love, enjoy, and honor it as a beautifully intimate gift from Christ to us, and as an invitation to grow into ever deeper communion with him.

11. While Herbert avoids overt polemic in this poem, his approach aligns strongly with Calvin's theology of the Lord's Supper. Calvin is clear that elements remain bread and wine. The Holy Spirit lifts us up to where Christ is, rather than bringing Christ down into the elements. By the Spirit we are so intimately united to Christ in the sacrament that we are present to him and he to us, and he conveys his very self to us. This is what Herbert calls the grace that comes with the elements, and it nourishes and strengthens our faith, just as the bread and wine nourish and strengthen our bodies. For both Calvin and Herbert this means that the heart of the sacrament is union and communion with Christ. If the only doctrine you associate with Calvin is predestination, you might like to read his account of the Lord's Supper in his *Institutes*, bk. 4, ch. 17.

SCRIPTURE: 1 CORINTHIANS 10:16–17

DWELL

- Which words, images, or phrases from the poem stand out to you? Ask the Holy Spirit to speak to you through them.
- What thoughts, feelings, or actions are prompted in you as you bring the poem and the Scripture text into conversation with each other? Hold these promptings before God.
- What difference might it make to how you prepare for and experience receiving communion to focus on it as the gift of loving intimacy with Christ, and a taste of heaven on earth?
- In the Lord's Supper, Christ honors us as whole people—bodies as well as minds and souls. Reflect with him on what it means for you to honor him with your body.
- The focus of this poem is our personal communion with Christ. Other aspects of the Lord's Supper flow from this, such as our communion with those who share the sacrament with us and the call to share Christ's love with others. How might all of these facets of the Lord's Supper shape your discipleship?

PRAY

Father of all . . .
May we who share Christ's body live his risen life;
we who drink his cup bring life to others;
we whom the Spirit lights give light to the world.
Keep us firm in the hope you have set before us,
so we and all your children shall be free,
and the whole earth live to praise your name;
through Christ our Lord.
Amen.[12]

12. This is an excerpt from the second post-communion prayer in Holy Communion Order One from the Church of England's *Common Worship*, 182.

GOING FORWARD

Notice—and give thanks for—the work that God has been doing in you through this poem. Be attentive to any next steps God might be inviting you to take.

Antiphon (I)

An antiphon is a short musical chant used as a refrain (the "chorus" that we see in this poem). In addition, it can refer to a musical "call-and-response" in worship, which this poem also exemplifies. It is one of just a few of Herbert's poems to have been turned into a hymn, and one of the few that is filled with nothing but praise. Here we have exultant voices and joyful hearts in exuberant corporate and personal worship.

Cho.[1] Let all the world in ev'ry corner sing,
My God and King.

Vers.[2] The heav'ns are not too high,
His praise may thither fly:
The earth is not too low,
His praises there may grow.

Cho. Let all the world in ev'ry corner sing,
My God and King.

Vers. The church with psalms must shout,
No door can keep them out:
But above all, the heart
Must bear the longest part.

Cho. Let all the world in ev'ry corner sing,
My God and King.

1. Cho. stands for "chorus." This is the part that everyone says/sings.

2. Vers stands for "versicle." Versicles are usually divided up between the minister and the congregation or choir.

REFLECT

Let all the world in ev'ry corner sing,
My God and King.

Do you sometimes feel tongue tied when it comes to praising God, as if your words could never be good enough? Don't worry! You don't need to come up with anything elaborate or fancy! "My God and King" is just fine! These are simple, scriptural words that each of us can say for ourselves, while also uniting our voices with people across the world. There are echoes here of the many times that the psalmist summons the whole earth to rejoice and sing praise to God (e.g., Psalms 98:4–9; 100:1). With the Psalms, we can even think of Herbert's words as a summons to the whole of creation, so that our voices join the chorus of praise from all creation too.

What's more, we never need to worry that God is too lofty and far away to hear us. As the first versicle assures us, we can be confident that our words fly up to God as part of a beautiful cycle: As praise ascends to heaven, so it continues to grow on earth, ready to ascend to heaven again.

There's also something rather countercultural for us about this poem, although it's easy to miss it. Almost everything is about what happens in a church service. These days many of us don't necessarily prioritize gathering with others for worship, for all sorts of reasons, including that many people have been deeply hurt by their experiences of church. Even so, there is food for thought in how this poem points us to what happens when we worship together.

For Herbert's first readers, even the poem's structure would have brought to mind a very familiar aspect of church services: the back-and-forth responses between the minister and the congregation or choir that are so characteristic of services in the Book of Common Prayer. Also, there are echoes of the opening of Psalm 95, which people heard every Sunday morning, and which Herbert would have said as part of Morning Prayer every day. This psalm summons everyone to rejoice and sing praise to God the King in whose hands "are all the corners of the earth" (1662 BCP).

Even when Herbert mentions that worship needs to flow above all from the heart at the end of the second versicle (echoing Ephesians 5:19, which encourages us to sing psalms, hymns, and spiritual songs in our hearts to God), this isn't just about our private, inward worship. He also says that we should be singing our hearts out in gathered worship, loud enough to be heard through closed doors! In Herbert's time, there were no congregational hymns. The only music the people sang in church was settings of the psalms. Some people looked down on this as uncouth: musically untrained people raucously bellowing out clumsy paraphrases of the psalms to pedestrian tunes. Herbert was a very gifted musician who dearly loved services with sophisticated choral music, but he was no musical snob. He knew how powerful and how spiritually formative it is for all of us to sing to the Lord together.

When you next join with others in worship, I hope you are able to sing along with all the hymns and songs! This poem is a reminder that you don't need to worry about your voice not being "good enough," just like you don't need to worry about whether you have "good enough" words to praise God. Just go for it!

SCRIPTURE: PSALM 95:1–7

DWELL

- Which words, images, or phrases from the poem stand out to you? Ask the Holy Spirit to speak to you through them.
- What thoughts, feelings, or actions are prompted in you as you bring the poem and the Scripture text into conversation with each other? Hold these promptings before God.
- This is one of Herbert's most confident poems. Ask God to help you to pray (and live) in the spirit of this poem, with its heartfelt, almost childlike, simplicity and enthusiasm.
- In our prayer life, we can tend to focus most on petitions (asking God for things) and intercessions (praying for particular people and situations). How might you incorporate more praise into your prayers?
- This poem summons us to whole-hearted, full-throated praise. When you next join in corporate worship, don't hold back with your singing! As John Wesley put it (quoting the 1662 BCP translation of Psalm 33:3): "Sing *lustily* and with a good courage. Beware of singing as if you were half dead, or half asleep, but lift up your voice with strength."[3]

3. John Wesley, preface to *Sacred Melody* (1761): https://reformedworship.org/resource/concern-manner-singing-john-wesleys-directions-leading-congregational-singing.

PRAY

We praise thee, O God: we acknowledge thee to be the Lord.
All the earth doth worship thee: the Father everlasting.
To thee all Angels cry aloud: the heavens and all the powers therein.
To thee Cherubin and Seraphin: continually do cry,
Holy, Holy, Holy: Lord God of Sabaoth;
Heaven and earth are full of the Majesty: of thy glory.
The glorious company of the Apostles praise thee.
The goodly fellowship of the Prophets: praise thee.
The noble army of Martyrs: praise thee.
The holy Church throughout all the world: doth acknowledge thee;
The Father: of an infinite Majesty;
Thine honourable, true: and only Son;
also the Holy Ghost: the Comforter. . . .
Glory be to the Father, and to the Son and to the Holy Ghost,
as it was in the beginning, is now, and ever shall be,
world without end. Amen.[4]

GOING FORWARD

Notice—and give thanks for—the work that God has been doing in you through this poem. Be attentive to any next steps God might be inviting you to take.

4. This prayer is the opening of the Te Deum (a very ancient Latin hymn), with a traditional doxology (expression of praise) added at the end. I've used the 1662 BCP translation, where it is part of Morning Prayer. You might like to look up the whole hymn.

The Temper (I)

In Herbert's time, "tempering" signified the process of tuning a musical instrument, as well as strengthening metals through heating and cooling. He draws on both of those meanings here as he wrestles with the experience of spiritual tempering. While he expresses his trust in God's process—it does indeed strengthen us and attune us more fully to him—he acknowledges that sometimes it can feel like we are being stretched and tested almost to breaking point.

How should I praise thee, Lord! How should my rhymes
Gladly engrave thy love in steel,
If what my soul doth feel sometimes,
My soul might ever feel!

Although there were some forty heav'ns, or more,[1]
Sometimes I peer above them all;
Sometimes I hardly reach a score;[2]
Sometimes to hell I fall.

O rack me not to such a vast extent;
Those distances belong to thee:
The world's too little for thy tent,
A grave too big for me.

1. In Jewish thought there were multiple "levels" of heaven. The number most often mentioned (in the Talmud, but not in the Bible) is seven, but some sources suggest many more. Paul mentions being caught up to the third heaven in 2 Corinthians 12:2.

2. A score signifies twenty.

Wilt thou meet arms with man,[3] that thou dost stretch
A crumb of dust from heav'n to hell?[4]
Will great God measure with a wretch?[5]
Shall he thy stature spell?[6]

O let me, when thy roof my soul hath hid,
O let me roost and nestle there:[7]
Then of a sinner thou art rid,
And I of hope and fear.

Yet take thy way; for sure thy way is best:
Stretch or contract me, thy poor debtor:
This is but tuning of my breast,
To make the music better.

Whether I fly with angels, fall with dust,
Thy hands made both, and I am there;[8]
Thy power and love, my love and trust,
Make one place ev'rywhere.

3. This phrase could have many different meanings, and Herbert probably intends to imply all of them! So, for example, "meeting arms" could signify an embrace, or a wrestling match, or even a duel, with arms meaning swords.

4. Herbert is recalling Genesis 2:7 here. We are mere dust creatures, whom God is stretching beyond our capacity to endure.

5. "Measure" means compare sizes with.

6. This line means "Can human beings truly express (or contemplate) God's vastness?" But lurking here is also an ironic reference to the incarnation. The "he" can also refer to God, and he *has* spelled our stature, so to speak. The eternal Son has come to us as a human being.

7. See Psalm 84:3: "Yea, the sparrows hath found her an house, the swallow a nest where she may bear her young: even thy altars, O Lord of Hosts, my King and my God" (1662 BCP).

8. "I am there" means I am in your hands (the hands of the one who made both angels and dust).

REFLECT

O rack me not to such a vast extent

Does your walk with God encompass the dramatic extremes that we find in this poem? As well as the equivalent of metals undergoing heating and cooling, and the tightening of strings on a musical instrument to tune them, the spiritual tempering process is even described in terms of being stretched on the rack, which was an instrument of torture. If that is how your relationship with God feels sometimes, reading this poem can be a "Thank God!" moment of relief. It's not just me! Someone else knows what this is like, and can give us words both to describe the experience and to help us to trust God in the midst of it.

For others of us, though, our relationship with God has a much less dramatic range. Yes, there are ups and downs, but nothing quite like this. Our experience might be more like the previous poem, where whatever distance there is between heaven and earth is bridged by praise, rather than our relationship with God leaving us feeling like we are being stretched almost beyond endurance.

The intensity of the extremes that Herbert describes in this poem might make us feel uncomfortable, and perhaps even inadequate. We might find ourselves wondering if we are truly "spiritual" if we can't pinpoint experiences like these in our own walk with God. I am one of those people. I can think of only a few times in my life when I have felt anything like the exaltation or desolation that Herbert depicts here.

Perhaps it's worth remembering that different metals need to be tempered in different ways for different purposes, and that each musical instrument has its own process for tuning. We can trust our gracious and loving God to spiritually temper us in ways that are best suited for our individual temperaments and our unique lives.

And don't miss the hidden presence of Christ in the fourth stanza! This is the pivot of the whole poem—three stanzas before it, and three stanzas after. On the surface it is a series of questions to God, but Christ himself is the answer to all of them. In Christ, God *has* met arms with us to embrace us. He has come from heaven to earth for us. He has descended into hell for us, risen again for us, and ascended into heaven for us. In coming to us as one of us he has indeed taken the measure of sinful humanity and does indeed know what it means to "spell our stature." This is why we can trust wholly in his love throughout the process of spiritual tempering, whatever that feels like for us.

Psalm 139:7–12 will be our scriptural conversation partner for this poem. I agree with those who think that Herbert might well have had this psalm in mind as he wrote it, especially verse 7: "If I climb up to heaven, thou are there: if I go down to hell, thou art there also" (1662 BCP). These words help us to hold onto the reassurance with which the poem ends. Wherever we find ourselves, physically and in our spiritual lives, we can trust that our loving God is there with us. This is why, as Herbert puts it: "Thy power and love, my love and trust, / Make one place ev'rywhere."

SCRIPTURE: PSALM 139:7–12

DWELL

- Which words, images, or phrases from the poem stand out to you? Ask the Holy Spirit to speak to you through them.
- What thoughts, feelings, or actions are prompted in you as you bring the poem and the Scripture text into conversation with each other? Hold those promptings before God.
- Reflect on the overall shape of your relationship with God. Has your experience been mostly relatively stable, or more like the spiritual roller coaster that Herbert is describing here? What are some of the ways that God has "tempered" you—strengthened your relationship with him and made you more "in tune" with him?
- Are there ways that the Lord is stretching you beyond your comfort zone in this season of your life? Does that make your heart soar? Does it make you afraid? Or both, or . . . something else? Seek to be as honest in your response to how the Lord is stretching you as Herbert is in this poem.
- The close of this poem reminds us that no matter what we feel or don't feel, and no matter where we find ourselves in our lives and in our relationship with God, we can trust that God has us in his hands. Ask the Holy Spirit to help you to trust in the loving presence of God through the tempering process, even when you wish it could all feel very different.

PRAY

Have thine own way, Lord,
have thine own way.
Thou art the potter,
I am the clay.
Mold me and make me
after thy will,
while I am waiting,
yielded and still.[9]

GOING FORWARD

Notice—and give thanks for—the work that God has been doing in you through this poem. Be attentive to any next steps God might be inviting you to take.

9. This is the first stanza of a hymn written by Adelaide Pollard in 1906: https://hymnary.org/text/have_thine_own_way_lord.

Employment (I)

This is one of several poems in which Herbert expresses his unhappiness with a life that he fears is pointless and unproductive. It is a prayer born out of discouragement, as he pleads with God to be able to bear good fruit, now and for eternity.

  If as a flower doth spread and die,
  Thou wouldst extend me to some good,
Before I were by frost's extremity
                    Nipt in the bud;

  The sweetness and the praise were thine;
  But the extension and the room,
Which in thy garland I should fill, were mine
                    At thy great doom.[1]

  For as thou dost impart thy grace,
  The greater shall our glory be.
The measure of our joys is in this place,
                    The stuff with thee.[2]

1. The "great doom" is the last judgment. The image is of Herbert being able to take his place among the redeemed, like a flower in the garland of praise to God.

2. The idea in this stanza is that we receive a foretaste of our eternal joy here (the "measure of our joys"), but we will experience the "stuff" (the substance/full reality of it) when we are with God. Herbert also echoes the parable of the talents (Matthew 25:14–30), where our eternal glory will be "measured" in relation to how we make use of the grace we are given.

Let me not languish then, and spend
A life as barren to thy praise,
As is the dust, to which that life doth tend,
But with delays.[3]

All things are busy; only I
Neither bring honey with the bees,
Nor flowers to make that, nor the husbandry
To water these.[4]

I am no link of thy great chain,[5]
But all my company is a weed.
Lord place me in thy consort; give one strain
To my poor reed.[6]

REFLECT

I am no link of thy great chain

Have you experienced a time in your life when you felt useless, and it seemed like your life was going nowhere? As the biographical sketch in the introduction indicates, Herbert went through a season of deep disappointment and uncertainty when he was in his thirties, when his hopes for his career seemed to have fallen through, he was often ill, and he didn't know what to do next. This poem might well reflect that time. As he puts it here, he is neither a flower, nor a bee who makes honey from its pollen, nor even the gardener who waters the flower. He feels unlinked from the chain that joins all created things to God. It seems that there is a place for everything with everything in its place, all doing useful things . . . except for him.

3. Everything about our life is only delaying the inevitable: the trajectory of life is toward the dust of death.

4. "That" refers to honey, and "these" to flowers, so the poet neither brings flowers for the bees to make honey, nor has the industry to water them.

5. The Great Chain of Being was the idea that all creatures had their particular place and function under God.

6. A consort is an ensemble of musical instruments. A strain is a melody, and a reed refers to a reeded wind instrument, but can also refer to a shepherd's pipe (a panpipe made of reeds). The shepherd's pipe or "reed" is a symbol for poetry, so this closing line could also hint at Herbert's desire to be given inspiration for his poems.

Herbert is well aware that everything we do in this life is fleeting. The opening image of a flower that blooms and dies is a common symbol for the brevity of life. But to switch the horticultural metaphor, Herbert also knows that branches in the Lord's vine are supposed to bear fruit, and there are consequences if they don't (John 15:1–7). Herbert is afraid that rather than being a flower that, by grace, will belong in God's eternal garland, he will be cast out as a weed.

There is a fine line to tread here. We want to feel like we are doing useful things in the world, to the praise and glory of God. But we also know that we can't earn our way to salvation by what we do, and neither can we make ourselves bear fruit for the Lord. This poem is Herbert's prayer for God by his grace to open the way to something good for him to do. Any possibility for his life—and ours—to blossom will have to come from God.

If we see the final lines not only as a musical reference, but also as a metaphor for poetry (see the explanatory note) then there might be a quiet turn at the end. After all, the Lord *has* given him a melody, although a mournful one. His struggle to see any worth in himself and his life has blossomed into this poem. Our next poem will pick up on this idea.

SCRIPTURE: EPHESIANS 2:8–10

DWELL

- Which words, images, or phrases from the poem stand out to you? Ask the Holy Spirit to speak to you through them.
- What thoughts, feelings, or actions are prompted in you as you bring the poem and the Scripture text into conversation with each other? Hold these promptings before God.
- Have you had times when you have had no idea what to do next and had to rely totally on God to provide a way forward? Take your fears, frustrations, and longings from that experience to God. If this is in the past for you, thank God for how he has led you into a new season of life. If you are feeling like this now, ask for a renewed sense of trust and hope.
- If we aren't careful, we can find ourselves either thinking that we earn our worth before God by what we do or just drifting along without caring whether we are rightly using the gifts God has given us. Do you

incline toward one or other of these—or both, depending on what is happening in your life? Reflect on this with the Lord and ask for his help to avoid both of these false paths.

- What kinds of experiences have led you to feel like your life is barren of praise to God, and dry as dust? What kinds of things have made you feel fully alive and attuned to God, and as though your life is blossoming? Ask the Holy Spirit what he might have to teach you through your responses.

PRAY

Gracious God, help me to trust
that you are at work in me,
to accomplish your will in and for me.
Help me to be faithful when I can't see the way ahead.
Set me free from my fears.
Set me free for whatever you call me to do,
whenever you call me to do it.
In Jesus' name. Amen.[7]

GOING FORWARD

Notice—and give thanks for—the work that God has been doing in you through this poem. Be attentive to any next steps God might be inviting you to take.

7. I wrote this prayer as part of my response to "Employment (I)" when I journaled my way through Herbert's poetry.

The Quiddity

"Quiddity" isn't a word we're likely to come across these days! It refers to the essence of something, but can also refer to quibbling—petty complaints or disputes. Herbert is playing on both meanings here. People who see wealth and power as the only measure of success in life would quibble about the value of poetry. For Herbert, though, the essence of poetry is that when he is writing it, he is with God. Nothing else in all the world matters more than that.

My God, a verse is not a crown,
No point of honour, or gay suit,[1]
No hawk,[2] or banquet, or renown,
Nor a good sword, nor yet a lute:

It cannot vault, or dance, or play;[3]
It never was in France or Spain;
Nor can it entertain the day
With a great stable or demain:[4]

It is no office, art, or news,[5]
Nor the Exchange, or busy Hall;[6]

---

1. "Gay suit" means bright clothing.

2. A hawk is mentioned on Herbert's list of status symbols because hunting with hawks was a popular pastime for the wealthy in Herbert's day.

3. "Vault" means leap; "play" means to act in a play.

4. "Demain" means an estate belonging to a manor house.

5. "Office" signifies a position; "art" means skill in a trade.

6. The Royal Exchange was the first shopping arcade in London; Westminster Hall in London was where the major law courts conducted business.

But it is that which while I use[7]
I am with thee, and *Most take all.*[8]

REFLECT

But it is that which while I use
I am with thee

This is a playful poem, but lurking not far below the surface is a painful experience that is common to many of us: the feeling that we are being judged and found wanting. Perhaps someone has insinuated that you haven't done very well for yourself in life. Perhaps someone has belittled something you're good at, or that matters deeply to you. Perhaps you don't need anyone else to do this. You might well have your own inner critic to nag you about all the ways you fall short.

Herbert knew all about this kind of thing, and he seems to have had a very persistent inner critic. In our previous poem we saw his frustration about feeling worthless and useless. In other poems, we sense his disappointment that he hasn't managed to achieve the kind of career success for which he had hoped. Herbert had his external critics too. After he finally did find fulfillment in returning to his original calling to church ministry, some people felt that he had wasted the advantages he had been given because he ended up as an obscure pastor in a rural parish.

In this poem, though, Herbert turns the tables on the critics. At first it all looks very self-deprecating, with his long list of examples of how poetry is seemingly inadequate. By implication, this is also a list of the kinds of things that the inner and outer critics would say make for a successful life. So, for example, he ought to have fine clothes and a large estate where he can host his friends for hunting and feasting. He ought to be physically strong, and to have travelled overseas. And if he couldn't manage any of that, well, at least he could have been a wealthy merchant with goods for sale in the biggest shopping mall in London (the Royal Exchange) or a high-flying lawyer on the circuit at the biggest courts (at Westminster Hall).

Herbert is right. Poetry is none of these things. You can almost hear the critics scoff. But the critics aren't the audience here. Herbert is not

7. "While I use" means while I am doing it (in other words, the process of writing poems).

8. "Most take all" is the equivalent of "Winner take all" in, e.g., a card game.

addressing them. He is addressing God, and it is God's opinion that counts, not theirs.

In a way, this poem could be seen as a response to the previous one, where Herbert was anxious about his life being pointless and useless. Here, Herbert realizes that for him, to write poetry is to experience the intimate presence of God. This outweighs everything else that would supposedly indicate a "successful" life. A truly successful life is not measured by the outward trappings of wealth and power. It is to be found in nearness to God. And so, for Herbert, writing poetry beats all the other cards in the deck—and the winner takes all.

SCRIPTURE: PSALM 49:12–20

DWELL

- Which words, images, or phrases from the poem stand out to you? Ask the Holy Spirit to speak to you through them.
- What thoughts, feelings, or actions are prompted in you as you bring the poem and the Scripture text into conversation with each other? Hold those promptings before God.
- Even if the specifics are of his time, the themes in Herbert's list of things that supposedly make for a successful life are familiar: wealth, power, choice of career. What might be on the list of your inner or outer critics to call into question your "success" in life? And how might this poem help you to re-evaluate what "success" means for you?
- Bring to mind a time when you found yourself judging someone, or belittling something important to them. Reflect on why you responded in that way. Ask the Lord for a spirit of curiosity, generous listening, and kindness next time you are tempted to make a snap judgment about someone.
- What is something that brings you closer to God, even if other people might think it a waste of time? Perhaps it is poetry or writing. Perhaps it is gardening, music, bird-watching, taking a walk, doing some kind of art or craft, running, playing a sport, fixing things . . . ? Give thanks to God for your sense of his presence when you do it, and allow yourself to value it, even if others do not.

PRAY

Our God in whom we trust,
strengthen us not to care so much
about the opinions and expectations of others
but to make it our highest priority
that in whatever we do, we are with you.
Amen.[9]

GOING FORWARD

Notice—and give thanks for—the work that God has been doing in you through this poem. Be attentive to any next steps God might be inviting you to take.

9. This is my adaptation of a prayer by Thomas à Kempis (1380–1471).

The Holy Scriptures (II)

The more you spend time with Herbert's poetry the more you realize how much his heart and mind were steeped in the Bible. This sonnet reveals Herbert's wonder at the endless depths we discover as we continue to read Scripture, and to be read by it.

Oh that I knew how all thy lights combine,
        And the configurations of their glory!
        Seeing not only how each verse doth shine,
But all the constellations of the story.

This verse marks that, and both do make a motion
        Unto a third, that ten leaves off doth lie:[1]
        Then as dispersèd herbs do watch a potion,[2]
These three make up some Christians destiny:

Such are thy secrets, which my life makes good,[3]
        And comments on thee: for in ev'ry thing
        Thy words do find me out, & parallels bring,
And in another make me understood.

        Stars are poor books, & oftentimes do miss:
        This book of stars lights to eternal bliss.

1. One verse points to another close by, and they point to another ten pages away.

2. The idea here is that just as various herbs from different places come together to make healing medicine, so Scripture verses come together to tell us our story and our destiny.

3. "Makes good" means fulfills.

REFLECT

This book of stars lights to eternal bliss

Where do you turn when you seek knowledge and wisdom? In Herbert's day some looked to the stars—to astrology—to discover truths about themselves and the world, and to find guidance for living. Some people still do that today. Herbert tells us that the Bible is the true "book of stars," containing true "heavenly lights" to illuminate our way to eternal life, and true constellations to give us right knowledge of God and ourselves.

There is so much wisdom for all of us about how to read the Bible well in this poem. Herbert shows us that we are not only to seek to understand how each verse shines like a star to guide us, but also to see how each verse fits within its context, and within the Scriptures as a whole. As many of us know, the Holy Spirit shows us different connections every time we read. It is a lifetime's labor of love to keep on seeing the links between different parts of Scripture, and between Scripture and our lives.

This also means that to interpret Scripture well will lead to Scripture interpreting *us*. If you are anything like me, I sometimes read the Bible as a matter of routine, or to learn something, or to prepare for a sermon or a class, but I can sometimes try to avoid "getting personal" with Scripture. It is one thing to read Scripture for information. It is quite another to read it for transformation. As Hebrews 4:12 reminds us, the word of God is alive and active, sharper than a sword to judge the thoughts and attitudes of our hearts. Through Scripture we not only come to know more of who God is but also to see ourselves more fully and truly, so that "in ev'rything / Thy words do find me out, & parallels bring, / And . . . make me understood."

SCRIPTURE: 2 TIMOTHY 3:14–17

DWELL

- Which words, images, or phrases from the poem stand out to you? Ask the Holy Spirit to speak to you through them.
- What thoughts, feelings, or actions are prompted in you as you bring the poem and the Scripture text into conversation with each other? Hold those promptings before God.

- Psalm 119:105 tells us that God's word is a lamp to our feet and a light to our paths. Are there passages of Scripture through which the Holy Spirit has particularly spoken to you? Thank God for the light he has given to you through them. Turn to one of them again now and listen for whatever the Holy Spirit might have to say to you through it, and for any promptings to connect your chosen text with other places in Scripture.
- As this poem suggests, if we are to truly mine the riches of Scripture, we need both to dig deep into small sections and to get to know the whole Bible well enough to see how the various parts of Scripture connect to each other. If you tend to focus on small sections of Scripture in Bible study and prayer, consider following a calendar that will take you through the whole Bible over a period of time. If you regularly read through the whole Bible, consider choosing one book to focus on for a while.
- Be intentional about asking the Holy Spirit to teach you something about God and something about yourself in every Bible passage that you read. Then ask the Holy Spirit to show you how what you have read might lead you to become more like Christ.

PRAY

Heavenly Father, help us to dwell in your word,
to meditate upon it day and night,
so that what we read becomes part of us.
By the Holy Spirit gives us grace
so that the words of Scripture
not only bring understanding to our minds
but also shape our lives to your glory.
Through Jesus Christ our Lord. Amen.[4]

GOING FORWARD

Notice—and give thanks for—the work that God has been doing in you through this poem. Be attentive to any next steps God might be inviting you to take.

4. This is my adaptation of prayer by Origen (185–254) for use before reading Scripture.

Mattens

Mattens (Matins) is another word for the service of Morning Prayer. As a parish priest, Herbert prayed this service from the Book of Common Prayer every day. The church's liturgy mattered deeply to him alongside his own prayers. This poem is both a wonderfully personal prayer and a nod to the shared worship of his church.

I cannot ope mine eyes,
But thou art ready there to catch
My morning-soul and sacrifice:
Then we must needs for that day make a match.[1]

My God, what is a heart?
Silver, or gold, or precious stone,
Or star, or rainbow, or a part
Of all these things, or all of them in one?

My God, what is a heart?
That thou shouldst it so eye, and woo,
Pouring upon it all thy art,
As if that thou hadst nothing else to do?

Indeed man's whole estate[2]
Amounts (and richly) to serve thee:
He did not heav'n and earth create,
Yet studies them, not him by whom they be.

1. "Must needs" means have to; "make a match" means be bound together.
2. "Man's whole estate" means our whole role and standing in life. We were created

Teach me thy love to know;
That this new light, which now I see,
May both the work and workman show:
Then by a sun-beam I will climb to thee.

REFLECT

Teach me thy love to know

When you wake up, what are your first thoughts about? What does your morning routine look like? Left to myself, my mind rushes straight to my to-do list, and I find myself plunging headlong into the day's tasks as soon as my feet hit the floor.

This poem has helped to train me to start my day differently. With echoes of Psalm 139, where God discerns our rising and our lying down, and where we have the assurance that when we awake, we are still with him, Herbert starts his day with the awareness that even before he opens his eyes, God's loving presence surrounds him. As I have learned, it really does change the feel of the whole day when you are deeply aware of waking up into the love of God, and that he will accompany you into everything that the day holds.

Even so, do you find it hard to really believe that the infinite and eternal God, who has the whole of creation to govern, would truly walk with you in the details of your little life? Herbert echoes Psalm 8, where the psalmist asks what are human beings that God should be mindful of them, when he wonders why God would care so much about his heart. Hear the response of this poem as God's answer to you: You are beloved and cherished, as if God had no one else to love, and nothing else to do, other than to seek to draw you closer to himself.

Notice that we don't have to do anything to be loved by God. We simply wake up into God's loving presence. In return, though, how could we not want to walk in love and gratitude, with our hearts and lives more fully oriented toward God? Herbert gives us a simple hint for how to do that. The purpose of our existence is to serve God, and to come to know more of God and his love in and through all things. "How might I serve God and come

---

to serve God, and also, as Herbert goes on to tell us, to come to know God and his love more deeply. Herbert is echoing the second collect (short prayer) of Morning Prayer in the 1662 BCP, which addresses God as the one "in knowledge of whom standeth our eternal life, whose service is perfect freedom."

to know more of his love today?" could be a wonderful framing question to put at the top of every to-do list.

And then we have some sun/Son wordplay! We first encountered Herbert's favorite pun in his poem "Easter." Here we join Herbert in allowing a first glimpse of morning sunbeams to remind us that the Son is the light of the world (John 8:12) and the dayspring from on high who shines upon us with the mercy of God (Luke 1:78–79; the whole of Zechariah's song is part of the BCP liturgy for Morning Prayer, which Herbert would have said every day). But also, a beam is a piece of wood. The beam of morning light reminds us not only of Christ the Light of the world, but also of the cross, which is both how we come to know the love of God most fully and the ladder by which we climb to him.

SCRIPTURE: LAMENTATIONS 3:22–24

DWELL

- Which words, images, or phrases from the poem stand out to you? Ask the Holy Spirit to speak to you through them.
- What thoughts, feelings, or actions are prompted in you as you bring the poem and the Scripture text into conversation with each other? Hold these promptings before God.
- If it isn't already part of your spiritual rhythm, consider incorporating a time of turning to God at the start of your day. If you already come before God each morning, as well as offering your own personal prayers, consider using a liturgy for morning prayer from your church tradition or another. Through these shared words, you are joining your voice to the wider community of believers, past, present, and around the world.
- How might it change your perspective to begin the day with the awareness of the loving presence of God already surrounding you, and how God will delight to be with you and draw you even closer to himself over the course of the day?
- What difference might it make to think of each day as given to us so that we can serve God, and come to know even more of his love?

PRAY

> O Lord, our heavenly Father, Almighty and everlasting God, who hast safely brought us to the beginning of this day: Defend us in the same with thy mighty power; and grant that this day we fall into no sin, neither run into any kind of danger; but that all our doings may be ordered by thy governance, to do always that is righteous in thy sight; through Jesus Christ our Lord. Amen.[3]

GOING FORWARD

Notice—and give thanks for—the work that God has been doing in you through this poem. Be attentive to any next steps God might be inviting you to take.

3. This is the third collect (short prayer) for Morning Prayer in the 1662 BCP. Herbert would have said these words every morning.

Evensong

This is the last in a mini sequence of three poems. Our previous poem, "Mattens," was the first. In between them Herbert placed a poem called "Sin." With wry, gentle humor he is saying that this is the pattern of our days. We dedicate ourselves and our day to God each morning; we will inevitably sin over the course of each day; and then we come before God in penitence and trust at the day's close. As with "Mattens," Herbert is both offering a very personal poem and linking it to the daily liturgy of Evening Prayer.

Blest be the God of love,
Who gave me eyes, and light, and power this day,
Both to be busy, and to play.
But much more blest be God above,

Who gave me sight alone,
Which to himself he did deny:
For when he sees my ways, I die:
But I have got his son, and he hath none.[1]

What have I brought thee home
For this thy love? Have I discharg'd the debt,
Which this day's favour did beget?
I ran; but all I brought, was foam.[2]

1. This is a *very* dense stanza! We will unpack it somewhat in the "Reflect" section.
2. "Foam" means sweat.

Thy diet, care, and cost[3]
Do end in bubbles, balls of wind;[4]
Of wind to thee whom I have cross'd,
But balls of wild-fire to my troubled mind.

Yet still thou goest on,
And now with darkness closest weary eyes,
Saying to man, *It doth suffice:*
Henceforth repose; your work is done.

Thus in thy ebony box
Thou dost inclose us,[5] till the day
Put our amendment in our way,[6]
And give new wheels to our disorder'd clocks.[7]

I muse, which shows more love,
The day or night: that is the gale, this th' harbour;[8]
That is the walk, and this the arbour;
Or that the garden, this the grove.[9]

My God, thou art all love.
Not one poor minute scapes thy breast,
But brings a favour from above;
And in this love, more than in bed, I rest.

3. "Diet" primarily signified a daily allowance of food (there's a hint here of God giving us "our daily bread"), but it also referred to a day's journey. So God's "diet, care, and cost" implies his daily provision, his care for us on our daily journey, and the cost of our redemption on the cross.

4. "Bubbles"/"balls of wind" mean soap bubbles that float into the air and burst. In Herbert's time, bubbles were a symbol of triviality and transience.

5. The ebony box (reminiscent of a coffin) is the darkness of night, but also in the seventeenth century, beds could be fully enclosed. Search for "seventeenth-century box bed" online to see some pictures.

6. "In our way" means in our path.

7. Wheels are the mechanism of mechanical clocks.

8. The image here is of a ship, buffeted by winds during the day, and safely in the harbor at night.

9. In each of these lines "that" refers back to the day with its work and "this" to the night and rest.

REFLECT

My God, thou art all love.

Did you—or will you—play today?! Notice how, in looking back over the day with God, Herbert thanks him for play/leisure as well as busyness. I wonder if you need that prompt as much as I do? Let this be a gentle reminder that God intends our days to include play as well as work!

Above all, though, Herbert gives God thanks for his saving love. In the very dense second stanza, he says that in his love God chooses not to "see" the full extent of our sin because we would be destroyed if he responded to our sins in the way that they deserve (Psalm 130:3–4). What would you rather that God didn't see about you?

And then, perhaps with Romans 8:32 in mind, which tells us of how God did not spare his own Son but gave him up for us, it is as if, by taking upon himself all the consequences of our sin on the cross, the Son becomes more ours than God's.

We are not meant to take either of these statements as literally true. God does see our sins, and the Father and the Son are never separated, not in the incarnation, nor on the cross (in fact, as Romans 5:8 makes clear, the undivided love of God is never more powerfully displayed than in the saving work of Christ). These are provocative poetic words to get us thinking about the unfathomable depths of God's love for us.

After thanks and praise comes an honest review of the day. What do we have to show for all God's loving care toward us? We ran our race (1 Corinthians 9:24), says Herbert, but all we produced was sweat, and the equivalent of soap bubbles that are carried away and burst by the wind. In the grand scheme of things, we would probably have to admit that so much of what occupies our days ends up being exactly that: the equivalent of sweat and soap bubbles.

As many of us will know full well, though, reflecting on what has gone amiss in our day can become like a raging wildfire in our minds. Like Herbert, we need to hear God gently telling us "Enough is enough" ("It doth suffice"), as he summons us to close our weary eyes, and shut down our overactive, overanxious brains, and rest in him. We can hand over our anxiety about this day and the coming days to God. As the KJV puts it, "Sufficient unto the day is the evil thereof" (Matthew 6:34).

Herbert is mostly referring here to night and sleep, and being rested and re-ordered for the next day, but he is also quietly hinting at the end of all our earthly days in death and our resurrection on the last day. Between now and then, whether it is day or night, activity or rest, we can trust that every minute of every day we are held in God's love:

"And in this love, more than in bed, I rest."

SCRIPTURE: MATTHEW 11:28–30

DWELL

- Which words, images, or phrases from the poem stand out to you? Ask the Holy Spirit to speak to you through them.
- What thoughts, feelings, or actions are prompted in you as you bring the poem and the Scripture text into conversation with each other? Hold these promptings before God.
- If it isn't already part of your spiritual rhythm, consider incorporating a time of turning to God at the close of your day. If you already come before God each evening, as well as offering your own personal prayers, consider using a liturgy for evening prayer from your church tradition or another. Through these shared words, you are joining your voice to the wider community of believers, past, present, and around the world.
- Reflect honestly with God about the day: What went well, and not so well, in your walk with him? And then hand the day over to God, with a prayer to be able to live more fully for him tomorrow.
- At the end of the day, and maybe especially in bed, do you find yourself mercilessly turning over in your mind everything that has gone wrong, or that you could have said or done better? Ask God to close your eyes and bring you peace. Hear him saying to you: "That's enough now! Rest in my love!"

PRAY

> O God, from whom all holy desires, all good counsels, and all just works do proceed: Give unto thy servants that peace which the world cannot give; that both our hearts may be set to obey thy commandments, and also that by thee we being defended

from the fear of our enemies may pass our time in rest and quietness; through the merits of Jesus Christ our Savior. Amen.[10]

GOING FORWARD

Notice—and give thanks for—the work that God has been doing in you through this poem. Be attentive to any next steps God might be inviting you to take.

10. This is the second collect for Evening Prayer in the 1662 BCP. Herbert would have said these words every evening.

The Church-Floor

This is one of a series of poems in which features of a church become starting points for meditating on the kind of people we are called to be in Christ.

Mark you the floor?[1] That square and speckled stone,
Which looks so firm and strong,
Is *Patience*:

And th' other black and grave, wherewith each one
Is checker'd all along,
Humility:

The gentle rising, which on either hand
Leads to the Quire above,[2]
Is *Confidence*:

But the sweet cement, which in one sure band
Ties the whole frame, is *Love*
And *Charity*.

Hither sometimes Sin steals,[3] and stains
The marble's neat and curious veins:

1. "Mark you the floor?" means "Do you notice the floor?"

2. The quire is part of the chancel, which comes after the nave (the long section with pews facing forwards) in a traditionally shaped church. The chancel is often separated from the nave by shallow steps, and sometimes with a wooden or stone partition or screen.

3. "Hither sometimes Sin steals" means "Sin sometimes sneaks in here."

But all is cleansèd when the marble weeps.[4]
Sometimes Death, puffing at the door,
Blows all the dust about the floor:
But while he thinks to spoil the room, he sweeps.
Blest be the Architect, whose art
Could build so strong in a weak heart.

REFLECT

Blest be the Architect, whose art
Could build so strong in a weak heart.

Do you visit churches when you are traveling? Whenever I return to the UK, I always make sure to visit cathedrals, churches, and chapels, and to attend services if I can. Sometimes there is a guide on hand to offer tours. Imagine that Herbert is your church guide here, and then allow him to be a guide to another place of worship—yourself, as a temple of the Holy Spirit.

Like a good guide, he draws us in with his opening question. Who would notice the floor unless someone pointed it out to us? That said, perhaps we *would* notice a floor like this! I doubt whether many of our own churches have checkered black-and-white marble slabs, and neither did most churches in Herbert's day! But many Oxford and Cambridge college chapels did and do. If you can find an image of the interior of Herbert's college chapel, Trinity College, Cambridge, you will see the black-and-white marble floor, and even two very shallow steps up to the chancel (although these were added after Herbert's death).

As the final lines make clear, though, this isn't so much a tour of a church as a gentle summons to pay some attention to what the floor is like in the temple of your heart, so to speak.

The white slabs (Herbert's "speckled" squares—if you look at white marble, you'll see that it is often mottled) stand for patience, and the black ones for humility. These are two unspectacular but richly scriptural and important foundational character traits for Christians, and if we're honest, two of the most difficult to sustain in our day-to-day lives.

And then, if you sometimes struggle to truly accept that you are beloved of God, take heart from Herbert's next image. Many churches have steps leading up from the nave to the chancel (or, in more recently built

4. Marble was thought to release moisture.

churches, from where the congregation sits up to a platform). Herbert associates that with confidence—not confidence in ourselves but in the grace of God in Christ, by which God leads us to himself. Finally, love is the cement that holds the whole floor together.

In all of this, Herbert is picking up on the idea that all of us individually and together are being built into a temple with Christ as the cornerstone (1 Corinthians 6:19; Ephesians 2:19–22; 1 Peter 2:5). All the virtues that Herbert highlights—patience, humility, confidence, and love—point us to Christ. They are a call to reflect his character as the foundation of ours, and to place our assurance in what he has done for us. As the Holy Spirit continues to build us into a temple he cultivates these traits in us, and even those things that might otherwise damage the floor, so to speak, are turned to good. Tears of repentance will cleanse the stains caused by sin, and not even the dust of death can dirty the floor, because through death we will be swept up into eternal life with Christ.

SCRIPTURE: COLOSSIANS 3:12–14

DWELL

- Which words, images, or phrases from the poem stand out to you? Ask the Holy Spirit to speak to you through them.
- What thoughts, feelings, or actions are prompted in you as you bring the poem and the Scripture text into conversation with each other? Hold those promptings before God.
- Which of Herbert's scriptural virtues—patience, humility, confidence, love/charity—resonate most with you? Which do you need to ask the Lord to help you to work on, so that you can better reflect his character?
- In this poem, the very things that might damage or dirty the floor are turned to positives. What kinds of things stain your spiritual floor, so to speak? Ask the Holy Spirit to turn these things into ways to cleanse and strengthen your heart.
- Next time you enter your church's sanctuary, look around. Is there a communion table? A font? A pulpit or preaching lectern? Is there a Bible visible, or a cross? Are there clear windows or stained glass windows? Allow what you see to help you to prepare your heart and

mind for worship. Then extend this idea more widely, seeking to be attentive to what is around you at other times and places, and allowing what you notice to become a prompt for meditation and prayer.

PRAY

Triune God, send your Holy Spirit to kindle my heart
with the pure and purifying flame of your love.
Clothe me with love toward others,
and clothe me with humility in myself.
Help me to weep for the ways I fall short
of honoring the love you have poured out upon me,
and the good gifts you have given to me.
Give me a holy longing to live for you,
by the Holy Spirit make me a dwelling place for you
until I dwell with you eternally.
Amen.[5]

GOING FORWARD

Notice—and give thanks for—the work that God has been doing in you through this poem. Be attentive to any next steps God might be inviting you to take.

5. I wrote this prayer based on a poem by Bianco da Siena (c. 1350–c. 1434), best known in English as the hymn "Come Down, O Love Divine": https://hymnary.org/text/come_down_o_love_divine.

The Windows

Here is another in Herbert's series of poems about features of a church—this time, stained glass windows. Not all Protestants have appreciated them. Many were destroyed in the wake of the Reformation because they were felt to be an idolatrous distraction. In 1630, shortly after Herbert was inducted into his church, someone smashed a window in a parish church only five miles away. And sometimes we can deride "stained glass window" piety: a faith that looks good but is far removed from the messy realities of life. In this poem, though, stained glass windows represent how the gospel is revealed through us when our words and life align. Although Herbert is particularly addressing preachers here, what he has to say readily translates for all of us.

Lord, how can man preach thy eternal word?
          He is a brittle crazy glass;[1]
Yet in thy temple thou dost him afford
          This glorious and transcendent place,
          To be a window, through thy grace.

But when thou dost anneal in glass thy story,[2]
          Making thy life to shine within
The holy preacher's, then the light and glory
          More rev'rend grows, and more doth win;
          Which else shows waterish, bleak, and thin.

1. "Crazy" signifies of flawed, uneven, wonky, cracked.
2. Annealing is the process by which glass is painted and then fired.

Doctrine and life,[3] colours and light, in one
    When they combine and mingle, bring
A strong regard and awe; but speech alone
    Doth vanish like a flaring thing,
    And in the ear, not conscience, ring.

REFLECT

To be a window, through thy grace

Those of you who are or have been preachers have probably asked yourselves a version of Herbert's opening question many times. For those of you who aren't preachers, though, you might well have asked yourself, "How can I possibly share the gospel with anyone?" or "How can I let someone know I'm a Christian?"

We often feel hopelessly inadequate. We are anxious that we won't have the "right" words, and we are also painfully aware of the gap between what we say and how our lives come across to others. Left to ourselves we are like fragile, cracked, flawed windows. Every preacher will inevitably distort the Scriptures in some way. All of us will inevitably say things that are wrong or unhelpful.

Does that mean we should just stay silent? No! Because God can still take our inadequate, flawed words and convey something of the wonder and beauty of Christ through them. For all that we are indeed "brittle crazy glass," by God's grace we can still become a window of the gospel to others.

As this poem makes clear, though, there does need to be a correspondence between our lives and our words. Words on their own are "flaring things," like fireworks that give a colorful flash for a split second and then they are gone. But when Christ anneals his story in our lives—when not just our words, but also our lives are aligned to the gospel—we become like a color-filled stained glass window through which people see something more of him.

3. Herbert is echoing two prayers in the 1662 BCP: one in the litany, which asks God to illuminate all clergy with true understanding of his word, "that both by their preaching and living they may set it forth and shew it accordingly," and one in the communion service, asking that clergy might "both by their life and doctrine set forth thy true and lively Word."

To see the beauty of stained glass windows, though, you need light. If it's dark outside you can hardly make anything out. When the sunlight comes streaming through, the windows are transformed into dazzling, bejeweled color. The windows can't make that happen. They have to be lit by a light beyond themselves.

This is us, friends. None of us can make Jesus be present to anyone, any more than stained glass makes light happen. But each of us is a treasured, flawed, irreplaceable little piece of the vast stained glass window that is the whole community of believers down the ages, through whom the light of the gospel is refracted. When your words and your life, your story and God's story, come together, then you and your life become a window through which others can see something unique about the supremely beautiful, merciful, just, loving, good, and holy God whom we serve and adore.

SCRIPTURE: MATTHEW 5:16

DWELL

- Which words, images, or phrases from the poem stand out to you? Ask the Holy Spirit to speak to you through them.
- What thoughts, feelings, or actions are prompted in you as you bring the poem and the Scripture text into conversation with each other? Hold these promptings before God.
- In what ways do you feel fragile or brittle? Take these to God, asking him to strengthen you, and trusting that you do not need to have it all together for God to shine the light of the gospel through you.
- Do you feel more comfortable sharing your faith in words or by your actions? What might it mean for doctrine and life, words and actions, to be more closely intertwined in you?
- How might it change the way you think of yourself and your life to see yourself as someone through whom the light of Christ shines uniquely and with great beauty for others?

PRAY

Holy Spirit, by your power at work in me
may the light of the glorious gospel of Christ
shine in my heart,
transform my life,
and brighten the world
to the praise and glory of the Father.
Amen.[4]

GOING FORWARD

Notice—and give thanks for—the work that God has been doing in you through this poem. Be attentive to any next steps God might be inviting you to take.

4. This prayer is adapted with permission from the Benediction for Epiphany in the Church of Scotland's *Book of Common Order*, 599.

Trinity Sunday

Trinity Sunday comes after Pentecost Sunday in the liturgical year, eight weeks after Easter. The Trinity is one of the deepest mysteries of our faith, and Herbert has written one of his most accessible poems to help us to enter into it!

Lord who hast form'd me out of mud,
        And hast redeem'd me through thy blood,
        And sanctifi'd me to do good;

Purge all my sins done heretofore:
        For I confess my heavy score,
        And I will strive to sin no more.

Enrich my heart, mouth, hands in me,
        With faith, with hope, with charity;
        That I may run, rise, rest with thee.

REFLECT

That I may run, rise, rest with thee

Be honest—is the doctrine of the Trinity something you know you should believe, but you have no idea how to even begin to get your head around it, or why it matters for your life? You are not alone! Let Herbert come to your aid!

One of his tasks as a minister was to teach the core doctrines of the faith in a catechism class every Sunday afternoon. He must have been *superb* at this, given what he accomplishes here!

I wonder if he might even have taught this prayer-poem to his parishioners? It is easy to memorize. The words are simple, the rhythm is like a nursery rhyme, and the rhyming scheme is very straightforward. You might even think, "*I* could write a poem like that!" Spoiler alert: I don't think so! For all its simplicity, this is a poem that leads us to deeper knowledge and love of God as Trinity, to confession, and to a stronger discipleship, until that day when we come to rest in the fullness of the presence of the triune God for all eternity. Herbert does this in just three stanzas of three lines each (yes, there are threes everywhere in this poem)!

There is some very profound Trinitarian theology distilled in that first stanza. Herbert opens by addressing God as "Lord," and then goes on to describe what the Lord has done for him, and for us. In that way, Herbert is showing us that the Lord our God is one, and yet also three. It is the one Lord—the whole Trinity—who creates, redeems, and sanctifies, even as we may also emphasize the role of the Father as Creator, the Son as Redeemer, and Spirit as Sanctifier.[1]

At the same time as giving us a glimpse into God as Trinity, Herbert is *also* describing who *we* are: created, redeemed, and sanctified by the triune God. The whole of who God is has loved you into being, and is at work in you and for you. This is the heartbeat of the doctrine of the Trinity for us.

In response, the second stanza leads us to acknowledge how far we fall short of responding rightly to the wonder and beauty of who our triune God is and what he has done for us. Herbert speaks for all of us when, again in the simplest of words, he expresses his need for forgiveness, and his desire to live a better life.

Finally, he asks God to help him do just that. There are three sets of three in this third stanza—one per line. Echoing a well-known prayer of confession (that we have sinned in "thought, word, and deed"), he asks for God to enrich his *heart*, *mouth*, and *hands* with *faith*, *hope*, and *charity* (love), the great triad from 1 Corinthians 13:13. In just these two lines Herbert has summed up everything we long for in our whole life of discipleship:

1. For those who find the details helpful, Scripture makes clear to us that God is one, and also that Jesus and the Holy Spirit do things that only God can do. This means that the Son and the Spirit, as well as the Father, are fully divine. In theological language, God is one essence and three "persons." This is almost impossible for us to get our heads around, but the heart of it is that the one God is love to the very core of his being as the loving communion of Father, Son, and Holy Spirit. Herbert quite brilliantly depicts another key Trinitarian concept here: that the whole of the triune God is involved in every action of God, even as we sometimes emphasize one person for particular actions.

that our thoughts, words, and deeds might be saturated in faith, hope, and love.

There is one more group of three in the final line. The culmination of the poem, and of the whole Christian life, is that he (and we) might *run, rise, rest* with God. "Run" is a word often used in the New Testament to describe our earthly life with God. With that in mind, you might think that the order would be: "run" our daily race, "rest" (go to bed), and "rise" (get up the next morning). But no. Here Herbert gives us "run" (our earthly race), "rise" (our bodily resurrection on the last day), and "rest" (our eternal Sabbath rest with God [Hebrews 4:1–11]). In other words, the whole of our earthly *and* eternal life with God is summed up in those three carefully chosen and ordered *r* words!

So, there we have it! In these nine lines Herbert has pointed us to the glorious mystery of the Trinity. He has given us a summary of our true identity as those who are created, redeemed, and sanctified by the triune God. He has also given us the pattern for the whole of our Christian life: that every aspect of who we are might be brought more and more to share in and reflect the life and love of the triune God until we dwell with him forever.

SCRIPTURE: COLOSSIANS 1:3–8

DWELL

- Which words, images, or phrases from the poem stand out to you? Ask the Holy Spirit to speak to you through them.
- What thoughts, feelings, or actions are prompted in you as you bring the poem and the Scripture text into conversation with each other? Hold these promptings before God.
- Allow Herbert's summary of the triune God's wonderful work for us as our Creator, Redeemer, and Sanctifier to be a prompt for praise and thanksgiving.
- Join Herbert in very simply and straightforwardly acknowledging how you have fallen short of living into the fullness of all that the Father has done for us in Christ by the Spirit.
- Ask the Holy Spirit what might it look like for your heart, mouth, and hands to be made richer in faith, hope, and love this week.

PRAY

Father, we praise you.
Through your Word and Holy Spirit you created all things.
You reveal your salvation in all the world
by sending to us Jesus Christ, the Word made flesh.
Through your Holy Spirit
you give us a share in your life and love.
Fill us with the vision of your glory,
that we may always serve and praise you,
Father, Son, and Holy Spirit,
one God, forever and ever. Amen.[2]

GOING FORWARD

Notice—and give thanks for—the work that God has been doing in you through this poem. Be attentive to any next steps God might be inviting you to take.

2. A collect for Trinity Sunday from the Anglican Church of Canada's *Book of Alternative Services*, 346.

Affliction (III)

Unlike many of his poems that arise from the midst of distress, Herbert doesn't question or struggle here. Instead, there is simply a profound realization of the presence of Christ with him, as the one who has suffered for us and continues to suffer with us.

My heart did heave, and there came forth, *O God!*
By that I knew that thou wast in the grief,
To guide and govern it to my relief,
    Making a scepter of the rod.[1]
      Hadst thou not had Thy part,
Sure the unruly sigh had broke my heart.

But since thy breath gave me both life and shape,
Thou know'st my tallies; and when there's assign'd
So much breath to a sigh, what's then behind?[2]
    Or if some years with it escape,
      The sigh then only is
A gale to bring me sooner to my bliss.

1. The idea here is that what seemed like the "rod" of God's punishment has become a scepter—a sign of God's sovereignty and favor.

2. "Behind" signifies still to come. If he has expended so much of his life breath in the sigh, how much breath does he still have left? The idea in this stanza is that we have a finite amount of breath tallied up for our lives, and if sighs expend more of it than our regular breathing then they will become a gale to blow us all the sooner into eternal life.

Thy life on earth was grief,[3] and thou art still
Constant unto it, making it to be
A point of honour now to grieve in me,
And in thy members suffer ill.[4]
They who lament one cross,
Thou dying daily, praise thee to thy loss.[5]

REFLECT

I knew that thou wast in the grief

What circumstances in your life have wrung the words "O God!" from you? Sometimes that exclamation can be borderline blasphemous. Sometimes, it is a desperate prayer from the very depths of our being. Here, Herbert's desolate cry also brings him comfort and consolation. It becomes a sign that God is right there with him in the midst of whatever is causing him such deep distress, to "guide and govern" him and his circumstances, and to bring him relief (Romans 8:28).

A sense of God's presence and providence in the midst of affliction doesn't necessarily resolve the issue that is causing so much distress. There is no indication in this poem that the circumstances have changed, but there is deep trust in God's guidance and his loving presence.

In particular, Herbert leans upon the truth that in Christ God has walked the road of suffering with us and for us. On the one hand, that means we do not get a pass when it comes to pain and suffering. Suffering is part of life in general, and the Christian life in particular, as we walk in the steps of our crucified Lord (e.g., Romans 8:16–17). But it means everything to Herbert to know not only that Christ endured grief, pain, and suffering in his life on earth, but also that Christ continues to share in his people's grief, pain, and suffering now, as the one who is still truly God with us in the midst of whatever we are enduring. If we do not recognize that, says Herbert, not only are we missing out on profound comfort in the midst of

3. In Herbert's time, "grief" meant not only mourning or sadness but also pain and suffering more generally.

4. Just as Christ suffered during his life, so he continues to feel the suffering of the members of his body, the church.

5. When we acknowledge only his suffering on the cross but not how he continues to suffer in his people, we are failing to praise Christ as fully as he deserves.

affliction, but we are also failing to praise Christ as we ought for the depths of his love for us.

SCRIPTURE: 2 CORINTHIANS 1:3–5

DWELL

- Which words, images, or phrases from the poem stand out to you? Ask the Holy Spirit to speak to you through them.
- What thoughts, feelings, or actions are prompted in you as you bring the poem and the Scripture text into conversation with each other? Hold these promptings before God.
- It can be a powerful witness when someone who has been through a painful season is able to testify to God's providential care in the midst of it. Do you have a story like Herbert's, of how God was "in the grief / To guide and govern it to my relief"? If so, give thanks to God for his loving presence and guidance, and perhaps consider how you might be able to share your story to help and encourage others.
- We often find it uncomfortable to sit with others in their pain. This can lead us want to move too quickly to try to offer explanations, or to "fix" what is wrong. Ask Christ, who has shared our sufferings, to enable you to weep with those who weep (Romans 12:15) and to walk well with them when they share their feelings and experiences.
- In his poetry, Herbert responds in many different ways to difficult circumstances. Sometimes he is questioning, confused, and angry; sometimes, as here, he trusts in God's guidance and presence. Reflect on the range of ways you have responded to times in your life that have made your heart heave, and have wrung the words "O God!" from you. What has the Lord taught you through your various responses, and how has God comforted you?

PRAY

That You are continually holding me, sustaining me, loving me
Jesus, I trust in You.
That Your love goes deeper than my sins and failings and transforms me
Jesus, I trust in You.

That not knowing what tomorrow brings is an invitation to lean on You
Jesus, I trust in You.
That You are with me in my suffering
Jesus, I trust in You.
That my suffering, united to Your own, will bear fruit in this life and the next
Jesus, I trust in You. . . .
That You give me all the strength I need for what is asked
Jesus, I trust in You. . . .
That you will teach me to trust You
Jesus, I trust in You.
That You are my Lord and my God
Jesus, I trust in You.
That I am Your beloved one
Jesus, I trust in You.[6]

GOING FORWARD

Notice—and give thanks for—the work that God has been doing in you through this poem. Be attentive to any next steps God might be inviting you to take.

6. This is an excerpt from the Litany of Trust written by the Sisters of Life. For the full litany, see https://sistersoflife.org/litany-of-trust/.

Sunday

With many apologies to Herbert, I have shortened this poem in order to be able to include it. I wanted to share an extract from it because I think the themes are important for us in our hurried, harried world. I have included five of the nine stanzas, but you will readily be able to find the whole poem if you would like to read and reflect on all of it.[1]

O Day most calm, most bright,
The fruit of this, the next world's bud,[2]
Th' indorsement of supreme delight,
Writ by a friend, and with his blood;[3]
The couch of time; care's balm and bay:[4]
The week were dark, but for thy light:
Thy torch doth show the way.

The other days and thou
Make up one man; whose face thou art,[5]
Knocking at heaven with thy brow:
The work-days are the back-part;

1. A version of my reflections on this poem and the next ("Denial") appears in McDonald, "George Herbert."

2. Sundays are the fruit/culmination of this world and the anticipation/foretaste of eternal life.

3. An "indorsement" is a signature ratifying a document. As the day of Christ's resurrection, Sundays are the ratification of our salvation signed by Christ our friend in his own blood.

4. The "couch of time" is the place where time rests; "care's balm and bay" means the healing from and safe haven for our anxious concerns.

5. The image in this stanza is of the days of the week as a person. Sundays are the face, with the body released to stand upright, looking toward heaven. The other days are the rest of the body, back bent over with labor (and burdened by our sins too).

The burden of the week lies there,
Making the whole to stoop and bow,
Till thy release appear.

. . .

The Sundays of man's life,
Threaded together on time's string,
Make bracelets to adorn the wife
Of the eternal glorious King.[6]
On Sunday heaven's gate stands ope:[7]
Blessings are plentiful and rife,
More plentiful than hope.

This day my Saviour rose,
And did inclose this light for his:[8]
That, as each beast his manger knows,
Man might not of his fodder miss.
Christ hath took in this piece of ground,
And made a garden there for those
Who want herbs for their wound.

. . .

Thou art a day of mirth:
And where the week-days trail on ground,
Thy flight is higher, as thy birth.
O let me take thee at the bound,[9]
Leaping with thee from sev'n to sev'n,
Till that we both, being toss'd from earth,
Fly hand in hand to heav'n!

REFLECT

Thy torch doth show the way

What do Sundays mean to you? Attending worship at your church? Worshiping God in other ways? Is Sunday a day when you try to hit pause, or is it a working day for you? Or a day spent taking children or grandchildren

6. The wife of the King is the church, the bride of Christ.

7. "Ope" means open. In his biography of Herbert, Izaak Walton tells us that Herbert sang this stanza on the Sunday before his death.

8. He enclosed the light of his resurrection in Sundays.

9. "At the bound" means in a single running leap.

to and from sports and other activities? Have Sundays felt different to you in different seasons of your life?

In Herbert's time everyone was required to attend church, but there were fierce controversies about how people could spend the rest of the day. Should they be able to play sports and games or not, for example? Herbert doesn't directly refer to any of that. He simply gives us what is in effect a hymn of praise to the theological and spiritual significance of Sundays.

We are reminded that Sunday is the day of Jesus' resurrection—the day our salvation is signed and sealed by our dearest friend. (Herbert's favorite pun is lurking here: Sunday is Sonday, the day focused on Christ the Son.) As such it is both the ultimate fruit of this life and the bud which anticipates the fullness of our own resurrection and eternal life. It is also a time of rest from work and care. If our backs are bent, literally or metaphorically, with the burdens of work and anxieties over the rest of the week, on Sundays we are released to stand upright with our faces lifted to God.

Sundays are like a beacon of light toward which we travel in the rest of the week, and which lights our way for the week to come. They are like precious gems threaded on a bracelet to adorn the bride of Christ. They are our day for spiritual nourishment, just as animals know that they will find food in the manger (with a quiet nod to the birth of Jesus and Isaiah 1:3). They are a garden that Christ has made for us, filled with herbs to heal our hurts from the rest of the week.

Sunday is also a day of delight and exuberant joy. Where the other days drag along the ground, Sundays fly, and we fly with them. In the final stanza we have the delightfully weird image of Herbert jumping over the rest of the week, hand in hand with a personified Sunday, until together they leap into heaven.

I doubt that even the best Sundays leave us feeling quite like this! Herbert is setting out an ideal of what it might be like to have a day dedicated to the Lord. In his time, and still for many of us, Sunday is the natural day for aiming toward this. These days, though, that isn't possible for everyone, and even for those of us who join in worship on Sundays I suspect that much of the rest of the day looks and feels like any other.

What might it mean to cultivate a pattern of regular, dedicated Sabbath time, something like Herbert points us toward here? A time to come out from under the burdens we carry, stretch ourselves upright, and turn our faces toward Christ. A time to celebrate our redemption and to receive the gift of spiritual nourishment and delight. A time that could be a beacon for our lives, and a springboard to carry us toward the Sabbath rest of communion with God that will be ours in eternity.

SCRIPTURE: HEBREWS 4:9–11A

DWELL

- Which words, images, or phrases from the poem stand out to you? Ask the Holy Spirit to speak to you through them.
- What thoughts, feelings, or actions are prompted in you as you bring the poem and the Scripture text into conversation with each other? Hold these promptings before God.
- Has Sunday observance and/or the concept of "Sabbath time" been part of your spiritual life? If so, how has that felt for you? Routine? Life giving? Oppressive? Liberating? If not, what attracts you or makes you apprehensive? Take your thoughts to Christ, who summons all who are weary to come to him for rest (Matthew 11:28–30). Ask him to encourage you, and to bring healing if that is needed.
- If you are able to join in public worship and pause from your weekly activities on Sundays, how might the myriad images in this poem—from Sundays as jewels in a bracelet to medicine for healing our wounds—transform how you think about, prepare for, and enjoy the day?
- In this poem, Sundays are both "time out"—a release from the crushing round of demands and anxieties—and "time for" God. Look again at the close of the "Reflect" section. If something like this is already part of your walk with God, consider ways of refreshing your practices. If not, you might like to consider building an intentional pattern of "time out, and time for God" into your life.

PRAY

God of rest,
Today I make the active choice
To enter into your rest. . . .
I choose to tune out
Of demands and deadlines,

Of performance pressures,
Of flickering screens,
Of that which robs my soul of joy,
And the ways in which the world
Seeks to define and shape my identity.

I choose to tune in
To your affirmation and love . . . ,
To worship and your word,
To the enjoyment of that which fills my soul with joy
And reminds me of my identity in Christ
As a deeply loved child of God.
Amen.[10]

GOING FORWARD

Notice—and give thanks for—the work that God has been doing in you through this poem. Be attentive to any next steps God might be inviting you to take.

10. This is a shortened version of "A Prayer For Sabbath" from Christ Church London. You can find it via the "Resources" link on their website: https://christchurchlondon.org/.

Denial

As with so many of Herbert's poems, this is actually a prayer, but this time, as far as Herbert is concerned, it's a prayer into the void. It's a prayer to a God who doesn't seem to be there. This is a poem that is at once intensely personal in its desolation and also saturated in the lament psalms that cry out to God from the depths.

When my devotions could not pierce
Thy silent ears,
Then was my heart broken, as was my verse;
My breast was full of fears
And disorder.

My bent thoughts, like a brittle bow,
Did fly asunder:[1]
Each took his way; some would to pleasures go,
Some to the wars and thunder
Of alarms.[2]

"As good go anywhere," they say,[3]
"As to benumb
Both knees and heart, in crying night and day,
Come, come, my God, O come!
But no hearing."

1. The main image here is of a bow as a weapon, but also perhaps the broken bow of a musical instrument.

2. Alarms are drum and trumpet calls to battle.

3. In this line his thoughts are saying, "We might as well go anywhere," since God is not listening ("But no hearing").

O that thou shouldst give dust a tongue
To cry to thee,
And then not hear it crying! All day long
My heart was in my knee,[4]
But no hearing.

Therefore my soul lay out of sight,
Untuned, unstrung:
My feeble spirit, unable to look right,
Like a nipt blossom,[5] hung
Discontented.

O cheer and tune my heartless breast,
Defer no time;
That so thy favors granting my request,
They and my mind may chime,
And mend my rhyme.

REFLECT

Come, come, my God, O come!

Have you been where Herbert is in this poem? Praying your heart out, and feeling betrayed by the apparent silence and indifference of God? Herbert expresses his sense of injustice on behalf of all of us. God is the one who has made us for himself. He has given us, dust as we are, the ability to be in relationship with him and to cry out to him. And then it seems that he refuses to hear us.

Herbert is almost done here. His heart is broken, his poetry is broken, he's on the point of giving up on God and trying to live for God. Why not simply give himself over to illicit desires ("pleasures"), or take his chances of life or death by going off to fight in the horrific Thirty Years' War ravaging much of Europe at the time ("wars and thunder / Of alarms")? As far as he's concerned, he might as well go anywhere and do anything. It seems like God has abandoned him, so why not abandon himself? His heart is

4. He has been kneeling in prayer, and praying with all his heart, hence "My heart was in my knee."

5. "Nipt" means nipped by frost, causing the flower to droop.

in his knees in prayer all day, but what is the point of praying and praying when it seems like God isn't listening and isn't even there? Those middle stanzas especially, the ones that both end with "but no hearing," depict utter desolation.

In this poem, the brokenness isn't just in the content of the words. It is also in the structure. The poem is all over the place. The lines within each stanza are of different lengths, and if you try reading the poem out loud, you'll realize that in many lines, like the third ("Then was my heart broken, as was my verse") the stressed syllables are in the "wrong" places. It is quite literally a broken verse.

But it's the structure of the poem, even more than the words themselves, that gives us the quietly wonderful turn at the end. This is something that might be familiar to you from the lament psalms, which are very much Herbert's model here. In all but one of the lament psalms, no matter how desolate they are, there is a sense of answered prayer at the end. Herbert does this in the most beautiful way here.

To see what he is doing, we need to look at the rhyming scheme of the poem. The first four lines of each stanza follow the rhyming pattern *abab*. Because pronunciation was different in the seventeenth century it's easier to see this from the second stanza onwards. But the fifth line doesn't rhyme with anything. It sticks out. It jars. Again, this is broken poetry, mirroring the brokenness and despair of endlessly praying into the void. Herbert's prayers are hanging there like those last lines of each stanza, seemingly unheard and unresolved.

But now look again at that last stanza! Do you see what has happened? *The last line rhymes!* So, even as Herbert is pleading with God to please hurry up and respond to him, in these last lines the very structure of the poem is telling us: The Lord *has* heard! The Lord *has* answered! The rhyme *has been mended!*

When you need to pray this kind of prayer, you have Herbert as a friend beside you in the darkness, giving you permission to express your own very personal version of the lament psalms, as he has done here. And from out of the depths Herbert is also gently telling us, with the Psalms, "Hang on in there!" In God's own time, and by his grace, there *will* come a renewed sense of his presence, and an awareness of prayers heard and answered.

SCRIPTURE: PSALM 13

DWELL

- Which words, images, or phrases from the poem stand out to you? Ask the Holy Spirit to speak to you through them.
- What thoughts, feelings, or actions are prompted in you as you bring the poem and the Scripture text into conversation with each other? Hold these promptings before God.
- Has there been a time in your life when you longed for an answer from God, and a sense of his presence and love, but it seemed as though he wasn't there or wasn't listening? How did you feel? Bring those feelings honestly before God.
- Do you recall a season when you felt that God was absent and silent, but then later you realized that he was right alongside you and answering your prayers in ways you didn't recognize at the time? Reflect on this in prayer with God.
- Consider writing your own prayer/poem of lament.

PRAY

When all is dark
and doubts are magnified;
when faith grows weak
and I relax
my hold on you;
Lord, in your mercy
and the greatness of your love,
do not loose your hold on me.[6]

GOING FORWARD

Notice—and give thanks for—the work that God has been doing in you through this poem. Be attentive to any next steps God might be inviting you to take.

6. From "A Better World," in Banyard, *Heaven and Charing Cross*, 3.

Christmas (Part 1)

This is part one of a two-part Christmas poem, and it isn't quite what we might expect! If you look up the whole poem, you'll see that the second part is a much more conventional praise-poem for the day. This poem follows immediately after our last one. Do you remember how in "Denial" Herbert pleaded with a seemingly absent God to come? And how, at the end of the poem, it turned out that God was already there? This is a poem about how in Christ, God has already come to us—and also how he is always ahead of us, waiting to welcome us.

All after pleasures as I rid one day,
　　My horse and I, both tired, body and mind,
　　With full cry of affections,[1] quite astray,
I took up in the next inn I could find.

There when I came, whom found I but my dear,
　　My dearest Lord, expecting[2] till the grief
　　Of pleasures brought me to him, ready there
To be all passengers' most sweet relief?

O Thou, whose glorious, yet contracted light,
　　Wrapped in night's mantle, stole into a manger;
　　Since my dark soul and brutish is thy right,[3]
To Man of all beasts be not thou a stranger:

1. "Affections" means emotions or desires.

2. "Expecting" signifies waiting.

3. The idea here is that even though he has defiled his soul by his "dark and brutish" behavior, by rights it still belongs to the Lord, since the Lord is the one who made him.

Furnish & deck my soul, that thou mayst have
A better lodging than a rack[4] or grave.

REFLECT

Whom found I but my dear,
My dearest Lord

How is your "horse riding" going? Horse riding was a classic metaphor in Herbert's time. Proper control of a horse signified proper control over your life, and especially your desires, with the rider often identified with the mind or soul, and the horse with the body.

At the start of this poem, both poet and horse are lost and exhausted from all the "pleasure hunting." This is not how we might expect to find Herbert spending his days (let alone his Christmas Day!): hard riding and fast living. In the previous poem, he was thinking about running after "pleasures," and both there and here this is a loaded term. It doesn't simply mean "enjoyable things." It means acting on illicit desires, sexual or otherwise. This is probably a good time to remind ourselves that even though his poetry is deeply personal, we can't simply identify Herbert with his poetic personas. It would seem that Herbert *did* have some vices (he apparently had a temper, for example, and he seems to have been a bit of a fastidious snob when he was younger). As far as we know, though, debauchery was not one of them!

He pulls up at the next inn he comes across, to find none other than Christ already there, waiting for "the grief / Of pleasures" to bring Herbert back to him. That's such a telling phrase, isn't it? In Herbert's time, "grief" meant pain more generally as well as sorrow, so it is the sadness and the pain of pleasure that throws him back upon his dearest Lord—the one he truly loves, and the one in whom he finds sweet relief at last.

Have you been there? Or have people you love been there? Frenetically seeking happiness, or at least a brief buzz that might pass for happiness, in all sorts of places and in all kinds of ways. Out of control and exhausted. And how all those other paths we take to try to find ourselves and our happiness end up being distorted shadows of our truest love and our deepest longing.

4. Rack is another word for manger, but it also has connotations of the rack as an instrument of torture, which leads us to the cross and the tomb/grave.

And so the poem finally gets to Christmas, although it's still a rather dark "celebration" of it. It also moves from telling a story to becoming a prayer. First it is a prayer of adoration at the wonder of the incarnation—how the glorious light of the divine Son is contracted into the baby lying in the manger. Then it is a prayer of confession. Unlike the ox and ass who traditionally do homage to their infant Lord at the manger (taken from Isaiah 1:3), Herbert acknowledges how his "beastliness" has damaged a soul made for relationship with Christ. And finally, it is a petition, pleading for Christ to clear out the mess within him, to make him a more fit place for his dearest Lord to dwell. It is a prayer for all of us.

SCRIPTURE: LUKE 2:1–7

DWELL

- Which words, images, or phrases from the poem stand out to you? Ask the Holy Spirit to speak to you through them.
- What thoughts, feelings, or actions are prompted in you as you bring the poem and the Scripture text into conversation with each other? Hold these promptings before God.
- What direction do you take when you find yourself running headlong away from the Lord, and losing your way? Perhaps it is "pleasure" of one kind or another. But perhaps it's work. Or distraction. Or chasing after money, or influence, or the esteem of others. Hold whatever it is before the Lord and ask him to show you what is driving you in that direction.
- Imagine yourself into the scene from the poem: Jesus is in the inn at the end of an exhausting road that seems to be taking you further and further away from him. He is waiting for you not in anger but in love and offering not strident condemnation but sweet relief. What does it feel like to find him there? What happens next?
- What might it mean for Jesus to clear out the mess within you and to furnish and adorn your heart and soul in such a way that you might be a more fitting home for him (John 14:23)?

PRAY

O holy child of Bethlehem, descend to us we pray,
Cast out our sin and enter in, be born in us today.
We hear the Christmas angels the great glad tidings tell;
O come to us, abide with us, our Lord, Emmanuel.[5]

GOING FORWARD

Notice—and give thanks for—the work that God has been doing in you through this poem. Be attentive to any next steps God might be inviting you to take.

5. This is the last stanza of Phillip Brooks's "O Little Town of Bethlehem." You might want to sing the whole of this Christmas carol as you pray in response to this poem: https://hymnary.org/text/o_little_town_of_bethlehem.

The Pearl (Matthew 13)

This is one of a very few poems where Herbert specifically mentions a Scripture passage. In this case, it is Matthew 13:45–46, where the kingdom of heaven is compared to a merchant who sells everything to buy a pearl of extraordinary value. Herbert is helping us to reflect on what we might need to renounce in order to be fully "sold out" for the kingdom.

I know the ways of learning; both the head
And pipes that feed the press, and make it run;[1]
What reason hath from nature borrowèd,
Or of itself, like a good housewife, spun
In laws and policy;[2] what the stars conspire,[3]
What willing nature speaks, what forc'd by fire;[4]
Both th'old discoveries and the new-found seas,
The stock and surplus,[5] cause and history;
All these stand open, or I have the keys:
Yet I love thee.

1. The "head" and "pipes" imply the source of knowledge and the means by which it is disseminated; the reference to a "press" takes us to the image of a mechanical printing press and also a wine or olive press.

2. "What reason hath from nature borrowed" means the knowledge we acquire from the world around us, in contrast to how we come up with laws and political theories from the workings of our minds, just as a good housewife makes use of what is available in the house.

3. "What the stars conspire" means how the stars influence events on earth.

4. Some of what we can learn from nature is readily apparent; other things we have to force nature to reveal, e.g., by fire.

5. "Stock" is what is already in a merchant's warehouse (knowledge from the "old discoveries" in the previous line). "Surplus" means additional purchases (the things we learn from new discoveries).

I know the ways of honour;[6] what maintains
The quick returns of courtesy and wit;[7]
In vies of favours whether party gains[8]
When glory swells the heart and moldeth it
To all expressions both of hand and eye,[9]
Which on the world a true-love-knot may tie,[10]
And bear the bundle wheresoe'er it goes;[11]
How many drams of spirit there must be
To sell my life unto my friends or foes:
Yet I love thee.

I know the ways of pleasure; the sweet strains
The lullings and the relishes of it;
The propositions of hot blood and brains;
What mirth and music mean; what love and wit
Have done these twenty hundred years and more;
I know the projects of unbridled store;[12]
My stuff is flesh, not brass;[13] my senses live,
And grumble oft that they have more in me
Than he that curbs them, being but one to five:[14]
Yet I love thee.

6. The "ways of honour" means what it takes to be socially successful.

7. "Quick returns" are rapid rejoinders. "Courtesy" is both politeness and also the correct ways of engaging with social superiors, equals, and inferiors.

8. "In vies of favors," etc., means knowing who has come out best in doing and receiving favors.

9. "Glory" means the ambition for worldly glory, which molds the heart and shapes every gesture and glance ("hand and eye").

10. The "ways of honour"/worldly advancement bind us to the world with a lover's knot.

11. "Bear the bundle" suggests servants having to carry their master's bags. Seeking worldly glory leads to burdensome servitude.

12. "Unbridled" means uncontrolled—he knows what an uncontrolled collection of sensual desires can lead to.

13. "My stuff is flesh" means I'm made of flesh.

14. "Being but one to five" means that he has five senses to his one reason, which tries to curb them.

I know all these and have them in my hand;
Therefore not sealèd but with open eyes[15]
I fly to thee, and fully understand
Both the main sale and the commodities;
And at what rate and price I have thy love,[16]
With all the circumstances that may move.[17]
Yet through the labyrinths, not my groveling wit,
But thy silk twist let down from heav'n to me[18]
Did both conduct and teach me how by it
To climb to thee.

REFLECT

Yet I love thee

What have you had to relinquish in your life in order to make seeking the kingdom of God your priority (Matthew 6:33)? What do you still need to get rid of to purchase the pearl of great price?

Here are three "ways" that seem to lead to success or happiness, but that can turn us aside from following "the Way." Herbert puts an abrupt end to their temptations with his repeated refrain: "Yet I love thee."

Herbert's "ways" are personal, but they also reflect an ancient threefold summary of the temptations we all face, and which the baptism liturgy that Herbert knew well asks us to renounce: the world, the flesh, and the devil.

Herbert begins with the devil, so to speak: the attraction of knowledge and the danger of intellectual pride which have been a temptation since the

15. This is an image from falconry. In addition to using a hood, a hawk's eyes were sometimes sealed (sewn shut) to keep it quiet as part of its training. Herbert is a well-trained hawk, so to speak. His eyes are fully open to these attractions, but he still flies to God.

16. Commercial language dominates these lines: "main sale and commodities" means the sales made and the material advantages that accrue from them; the "rate and price" at which he has God's love is both the cost to Christ (the cross—we are bought with a price [1 Corinthians 6:20]) and the cost to himself (giving up the three "ways" of learning, honor, and pleasure).

17. "All the circumstances that may move" means all the possible variables merchants need to consider in their calculations.

18. The silk twist refers to the silk thread that led Theseus out of the minotaur's cave in Greek mythology, filtered through Calvin's use of the same image in his *Institutes*, where Scripture is the silk twist given to us by God to lead us out of the labyrinth of the world to salvation.

serpent's words to Eve in the garden. Herbert was a Cambridge academic. He knew both the benefits and the dangers of the pursuit of learning. As with each of the ways, something good in itself can become an idol because of our inordinate pursuit of it. Especially at a time when the internet gives us the "keys" to vastly more information than Herbert could have imagined, what are some of the temptations associated with the acquisition of knowledge for you?

Next we have "the world," in all of its "vain pomp and glory" (1662 BCP baptism service), set in another context that Herbert knew well: the sophisticated brutality of trying to get ahead at the king's court. What he describes is still painfully familiar. Can you come up with the brilliant response that will get you noticed and cut others down? Whom should you network with, as you calculate how to make the right impressions on the right people? If you do a favor for someone higher up the ladder, will they help you out? And then, is success worth the cost if you have to sell your soul for it (Matthew 16:26)?

Finally there is "pleasure," or unrestrained sensual indulgence. While we tend to think of "the lust of the flesh" only in sexual terms, it is the inordinate pursuit of anything that delights our senses. Even good things, when "unbridled," can end up becoming cravings that dominate our lives. What "desires of the flesh" hinder your walk with God?

Herbert tells us he knows all of these ways and has turned from them to God with his eyes open. With the parable of the pearl in mind, the language of a merchant's commercial calculations runs through the whole poem. He knows that forsaking these ways to buy the pearl is a bargain. After all, as Paul tells us in Romans 6:23, the wages of sin—of succumbing to the temptations of the world, the flesh, and the devil—is death. By contrast, salvation in Christ is the *gift* of God.

As this suggests, for all Herbert's commercial language, we cannot calculate our way to right relationship with God, and left to ourselves we could never muster the confident "Yet I love thee" to banish all the temptations we face. In the end Herbert acknowledges that it is not our "groveling wit" (our feeble intelligence) that will lead us from false paths back to God's ways, and salvation is not a carefully weighed transaction. All is grace. It is God's gift of letting down his "silk twist" to us (his revelation to us in Scripture, and his coming to us in Christ) that means we can come to know him, and learn to follow him. It is God himself who leads us out of the labyrinth of temptations and enables us to come to him.

SCRIPTURE: MATTHEW 13:45–46

DWELL

- Which words, images, or phrases from the poem stand out to you? Ask the Holy Spirit to speak to you through them.
- What thoughts, feelings, or actions are prompted in you as you bring the poem and the Scripture text into conversation with each other? Hold these promptings before God.
- Which of Herbert's three ways are the most dangerous for you: the inordinate pursuit of knowledge, worldly success, or sensual pleasure? How have you sought to combat them?
- Are there other "ways" that might be harmless or even good in themselves, but for which you are at risk of giving up the priceless pearl of the kingdom? These could be anything from shopping to sports to social media . . . Ask the Holy Spirit to show you what these "ways" are for you, and what it will mean for you to respond to them with "Yet I love thee."
- When in your life have you been able to recognize God's "silk twist" leading you out of wrong paths? In what ways do you still struggle to acknowledge that everything about your walk with God is a gift of sheer grace?

PRAY

> Lord, we beseech thee, grant thy people grace to withstand the temptations of the world, the flesh, and the devil, and with pure hearts and minds to follow thee the only God; through Jesus Christ our Lord. Amen.[19]

19. This prayer is the collect for the eighteenth Sunday after Trinity in the 1662 BCP. This collect was modified in 1662, so it is not the version that Herbert himself would have known.

GOING FORWARD

Notice—and give thanks for—the work that God has been doing in you through this poem. Be attentive to any next steps God might be inviting you to take.

Unkindness

In Herbert's time the word "unkind" meant unnatural as well as what it signifies for us today. In this poem he writes about something that none of us would willingly admit to, but if we're honest it describes a reality for us much of the time. We treat God in ways that we would never treat any of our friends. That is "unkind" in both senses of the term.

Lord, make me coy and tender to offend:[1]
In friendship, first I think, if that agree,
Which I intend,
Unto my friend's intent and end.[2]
I would not use a friend as I use Thee.

If any touch my friend, or his good name,[3]
It is my honour and my love to free
His blasted fame
From the least spot or thought of blame.[4]
I could not use a friend as I use Thee.

My friend may spit upon my curious floor:
Would he have gold? I lend it instantly;
But let the poor,
And thou within them, starve at door.[5]
I cannot use a friend as I use Thee.

1. He is asking God to make him reserved and careful about causing offense.

2. "In friendship, I first think about whether what I am intending to do is in accord with the intent and goals of my friend."

3. "Touch" means harm.

4. "Blasted fame" means damaged reputation; "spot" means blemish.

5. The contrast here is between how ready he is to lend money to a friend if he needs it, in contrast to Proverbs 19:17, which tells us that whoever has pity on the poor lends to the Lord.

When that my friend pretendeth to a place,
I quit my interest, and leave it free:[6]
                    But when thy grace
          Sues for my heart, I thee displace,[7]
Nor would I use a friend as I use Thee.

Yet can a friend what thou hast done fulfil?
O write in brass, *My God upon a tree*
                    His blood did spill
          Only to purchase my good-will:
Yet use I not my foes as I use thee.

REFLECT

I would not use a friend as I use Thee.

Herbert is onto something here, isn't he? We are careful to think about how what we say or do will impact our friends, and if someone maligns them, we spring to their defense. We are rarely as intentional when it comes to thinking about how our words and actions accord with our faith, or how they might affect the way others think of Christ and Christians. And if someone mocks Christ, do we speak up or let it slide?

And then, we cut our friends plenty of slack and we're as generous as we can be in helping them out. The poor? Not so much. With a text like Proverbs 19:17 in mind, which tells us that to have pity on the poor is to lend to the Lord, and also the parable of the rich man and Lazarus (Luke 16:19–31), this attitude is a problem for anyone who would claim friendship with Jesus.

Herbert then remarks that if we and our friend both desire a particular role or honor, we will step aside to allow our friend to have it. The Lord of all graciously asks for our hearts, and we push him aside.

The word "use" in this poem primarily means treat. Herbert is saying that he would not treat a friend—or an enemy—as he treats God. Even so, the word still carries connotations of us merely "using" God. No friend has ever done or could ever do what Christ has done for us, and yet we hardly give him a thought, except when we want something, or need him to help us out when things go wrong. Then we expect him to be at our beck and

6. When a friend is after a particular position, I withdraw from seeking it myself to leave the way clear for them.

7. To "sue" is to seek or ask for; to "displace" is to push out.

call. We also take for granted what Christ has already done for us, abusing that by presuming on God's forgiveness when we do what we know is offensive to him.

It's not difficult to work out how we would react if someone we thought of as a friend did this kind of thing over and over again in their relationship with us, and we would soon run out of friends if we treated them like this. Yet God graciously persists in his relationship with us. While we were yet sinners Christ died for us (Romans 5:6–8) and on the cross Christ extends forgiveness to those who put him there (Luke 23:34). Nevertheless, that is no excuse for the many ways that we are unkind—both mean spirited and unnatural—in our response to God. As our Scripture text for this poem reminds us, Jesus has indeed called us friends, and he also calls us to live toward him and others in ways that are fitting for that extraordinary gift of friendship.

SCRIPTURE: JOHN 15:9–17

DWELL

- Which words, images, or phrases from the poem stand out to you? Ask the Holy Spirit to speak to you through them.
- What thoughts, feelings, or actions are prompted in you as you bring the poem and the Scripture text into conversation with each other? Hold these promptings before God.
- Think about your close friendships. How do you maintain those? What kinds of things do you do—and refrain from doing—so that the friendship flourishes? How might you be as intentional about your relationship with God?
- Let Herbert's shrewd analysis in this poem become a prompt for you to reflect on how you forget, ignore, or merely use God. Acknowledge this with God in prayer and ask God to help you to live in ways that more fully honor his great kindness toward you.
- When we think about our relationship with God, we usually focus primarily on personal, inward things like our prayer life. Herbert reminds us that how we treat others, especially those who are less privileged than us, is also an indicator of the state of our relationship with God. Ask the Holy Spirit to probe your heart and your life in this regard.

PRAY

Beloved Savior,
how could I ever fully fathom your love for me?
Love to the loveless shown, that they might lovely be.
Who am I, that for my sake my Lord should take frail flesh and die?
You are my Friend, my Friend indeed
who at my need your life did spend
and in whose sweet praise
I could gladly spend all my days.[8]

GOING FORWARD

Notice—and give thanks for—the work that God has been doing in you through this poem. Be attentive to any next steps God might be inviting you to take.

8. I have borrowed most of the words for this prayer from the hymn "My Song Is Love Unknown" by Samuel Crossman (1623–83). I drew on this hymn for the prayers for "Redemption" and "The Sepulchre" too. Crossman loved Herbert's poetry, and this hymn is filled with echoes of it: https://hymnary.org/text/my_song_is_love_unknown.

Life

In this poem, Herbert offers us a gentle memento mori (a reminder of death), with some wise perspective on living well in the meanwhile.

I made a posy, while the day ran by:
Here will I smell my remnants out, and tie
My life within this band.[1]
But Time did beckon to the flowers, and they
By noon most cunningly did steal away,[2]
And wither'd in my hand.

My hand was next to them, and then my heart;
I took, without more thinking, in good part
Time's gentle admonition;
Who did so sweetly death's sad taste convey,
Making my mind to smell my fatal day,
Yet sug'ring the suspicion.[3]

Farewell dear flowers, sweetly your time ye spent,
Fit, while ye lived, for smell or ornament,
And after death for cures.[4]
I follow straight[5] without complaints or grief,
Since, if my scent be good, I care not if
It be as short as yours.

1. "My remnants" means the remainder of my life, and the "band" is the ribbon with which he ties the posy.
2. "Cunningly" means sneakily.
3. "Sug'ring the suspicion" means sweetening the reminder of his coming death.
4. Dried flowers were often used as ingredients in medicines.
5. "I follow straight" means I follow directly.

REFLECT

Farewell dear flowers, sweetly your time ye spent

I suspect that you are like me in that you don't generally think very much about the brevity of your life. If you are going to be confronted by a hint of your own death, though, it might as well be through the sweet scent and gentle end of a beautiful bouquet!

From the Bible and classical antiquity down the centuries to Herbert's time and beyond, poets have drawn on the image of flowers that fade to remind us of the beauty and brevity of earthly life, and to draw out a range of implications for how we live, from incentives to virtuous living to wanton hedonism.

Herbert's poem is very much part of the long line of literary reflection on flowers, but there seems to be much more to it for him than merely giving his own twist to a well-known tradition. No other aspect of the creation appears as frequently in his poetry as flowers. Later we will reflect on one of his best and most famous poems, "The Flower." Herbert genuinely seems to have delighted in flowers, receiving them as a gift of God for their loveliness, their usefulness, and the lessons we can learn from them.

As well as being sweet smelling and beautiful while they live, flowers are useful in death: After they wither they can become ingredients for medicines. Like many in his time, both women and men, Herbert was very interested in the curative properties of flowers and other plants. In fact, in his manual for pastors he commended this kind of knowledge as important for pastors, so that they could help people physically as well as spiritually.

This means that Herbert's flowers don't simply remind us of the inevitability of death. They give us hints about how to live well. Whether the time we are given is long or short, do our lives bring something beautiful and good to others? Do our lives bring something of the aroma of Christ to others (2 Corinthians 2:14–16), as flowers offer their beautiful scent? Will we live in such a way that there is a legacy of love and healing from us even after our death?

SCRIPTURE: ISAIAH 40:6–8

DWELL

- Which words, images, or phrases from the poem stand out to you? Ask the Holy Spirit to speak to you through them.
- What thoughts, feelings, or actions are prompted in you as you bring the poem and the Scripture text into conversation with each other? Hold these promptings before God.
- We don't like to be reminded that our earthly lives are fleeting. Even if we live to a good old age, that is a mere blip in terms of earthly history, let alone our eternal life with the Lord. How does this poem help you to get perspective on both living and dying?
- Ask the Holy Spirit to show you how you might live more fully into the lessons Herbert learns from the flowers, so as to bring a sweet scent of Christ's healing, saving love to others.
- Herbert particularly seems to love flowers, both in themselves and for what they can teach us about God and ourselves. Is there part of creation that is the equivalent for you? For me, it is birds. Thank God for those aspects of his creation that particularly draw you in and draw you to God. Ask God to help you to continue to delight in them and learn from them.

PRAY

Because their work is so great, we pray,
O Father, your blessing on these small flowers . . .
May the strength of their fragile
beauty in bloom give pause to passers-by
who will meet in their sweet scent and radiant
forms whisperings of grace, stirrings of the
spirit, and the awakenings of eternal hungers,
that can be met and satisfied only in you.
Let these flowers, O Lord, bear witness in their
deepest natures to eternal things.

Let our lives also, O Lord, do the same.
Amen.[6]

GOING FORWARD

Notice—and give thanks for—the work that God has been doing in you through this poem. Be attentive to any next steps God might be inviting you to take.

6. This prayer is taken from the close of "A Liturgy for the Planting of Flowers," in McKelvey, *Every Moment Holy*, 90–91.

Submission

Here is a poem for all of us who have been absolutely certain that we have found exactly the right next step in our lives—a step up from where we are now, and one that accords both with what we want and what we think God wants for us. And then it all falls through . . .

But that[1] thou art my wisdom, Lord,
And both mine eyes are thine,[2]
My mind would be extremely stirr'd
For missing my design.[3]

Were it not better to bestow
Some place and power on me?
Then should thy praises with me grow,
And share in my degree.[4]

But when I thus dispute and grieve,
I do resume my sight,
And pilf'ring what I once did give,
Disseize thee of thy right.[5]

How know I, if thou shouldst me raise,
That I should then raise thee?
Perhaps great places and thy praise
Do not so well agree.

1. "But that" means if it weren't for the fact that.

2. The idea behind God having both his eyes is that Herbert is walking by faith and trust in God, not by his own sight, according to his own plans and desires.

3. "Missing my design" means not obtaining what I had planned on.

4. "Share in my degree" means share in my advancement to a higher position.

5. Herbert has stolen (pilfered) his eyes back from God—he is back to seeing things from his own perspective again. "Disseize" means deprive.

Wherefore unto my gift I stand;[6]
    I will no more advise:[7]
Only do thou lend me a hand,
    Since thou hast both mine eyes.

REFLECT

Only do thou lend me a hand,
Since thou hast both mine eyes.

Many of us will know Proverbs 3:5–6 by heart, about trusting in the Lord with all our hearts and not relying on our own understanding, submitting our ways to him, and trusting that he will direct our paths. It is fairly easy to hold onto these words when not much is at stake, but what about when your dreams go up in smoke? What about when you thought you really were on God's path for you, but then it all came to nothing . . . ?

In all likelihood this is a strongly autobiographical poem. Herbert had turned aside from his initial intention to enter the ministry to become the university orator, which he saw as a stepping-stone to high office. Nothing came of it, and this might well be a poem about "the one that got away." It gives us words for those times when we are hanging onto our trust in God by a thread. We find ourselves giving lip service through gritted teeth to having surrendered our wisdom to God's, when it seems like what God wants for us is nothing like what we want for ourselves. The image Herbert uses for this is that he has given God his eyes. He has committed to walking by faith, not sight, submitting to God's providence, rather than trusting in his own plans, desires, and perception of things.

He says that if it weren't for the fact that he has surrendered himself to God in this way, his mind "would be extremely stirr'd" about his plans falling through. It's very clear, though, that he is still very, very upset about it, and he continues to rehearse all the reasons why he thinks this is desperately unfair. Wouldn't God get so much more praise from him if he had the powerful position that he craves? It is very easy to persuade ourselves that we could do so much more for God, and be so much better disciples, if only we had greater power, prestige, authority, wealth, or whatever else we are chasing after.

6. He will stand by giving his eyes over to God.
7. He will stop trying to advise God about what is best.

While he is disputing with God and grieving the loss of what he had longed for, Herbert is effectively snatching his eyes back from God. He is looking at things from his own perspective again rather than trusting to God's good intentions for him. And he has to admit that God is right: if he had obtained what he had hoped for, it might well have driven him away from God, not closer to him.

Herbert gives his eyes back to God again at the close, surrendering his hopes and plans to God's wisdom. In the achingly sad final two lines, though, he pleads with God to lend him a hand to guide him, because God has both his eyes. He is walking on in the dark with no idea where to go next. As our Scripture text reminds us, sometimes we are called to walk on in darkness, trusting in the Lord to guide us, rather than trying to see by the light of our own making.

SCRIPTURE: ISAIAH 50:10

DWELL

- Which words, images, or phrases from the poem stand out to you? Ask the Holy Spirit to speak to you through them.
- What thoughts, feelings, or actions are prompted in you as you bring the poem and the Scripture text into conversation with each other? Hold these promptings before God.
- If you are in the midst of something like what this poem depicts, let Herbert help you to find the words to express what you feel as you ask God to lead you by the hand. If you have found yourself in this kind of situation in the past, reflect on how God brought you through it, and what that experience has taught you about yourself and what it means to trust in God.
- It can be very easy to confuse what we most deeply want with what we think God wants for us. What are the areas in your life where you find it hardest to discern in this regard? Your job? A relationship? A choice of school or career? Something else? Ask the Holy Spirit to help you to explore why you have found it harder to accept God upending your plans in one aspect of your life rather than another.

- Herbert uses a very striking motif throughout this poem: giving our eyes to God. It means being prepared to let go of how we see things in order to walk by faith and trust in God. What might it mean for you to give your eyes to God?

PRAY

O Christ in whom the final fulfillment
of all hope is held secure. . . .

What I so wanted
has not come to pass.
I invested my hopes in desires
that returned only sorrow
and frustration. . . .

So let me be tutored by this new
disappointment.
Let me listen to its holy whisper,
that I might release at last these lesser dreams.
That I might embrace the better dreams you
dream for me, and for your people,
and for your kingdom, and for your creation . . .

Not my dreams, O Lord,
not my dreams,
but yours, be done.
Amen.[8]

GOING FORWARD

Notice—and give thanks for—the work that God has been doing in you through this poem. Be attentive to any next steps God might be inviting you to take.

8. From "A Liturgy for the Death of a Dream," in McKelvey, *Every Moment Holy*, 232–35. This whole liturgy resonates deeply with Herbert's poem.

Justice (I)

This poem follows directly after "Submission," and Herbert is pondering similar themes. There it was with regard to a very specific disappointment. Here the issues are more general. Herbert helps us to be honest about how God's ways sometimes seem unjust to us, and then to be equally honest about ourselves.

I cannot skill of these thy ways.[1]
Lord, thou didst make me, yet thou woundest me;
Lord, thou dost wound me, yet thou dost relieve me:
Lord, thou relievest, yet I die by thee:
Lord, thou dost kill me, yet thou dost reprieve me.

But when I mark my life and praise,
Thy justice me most fitly pays:
For, *I do praise thee, yet I praise thee not:*
My prayers mean thee, yet my prayers stray:[2]
I would do well, yet sin the hand hath got:[3]
My soul doth love thee, yet it loves delay.
I cannot skill of these my ways.

1. "Skill of" means work out/understand.

2. "I intend to pray to you, but my prayers go astray."

3. Sin has got the upper hand. Romans 7:14–24 is behind this line, where Paul expresses what it is like to want to do good but to end up doing the sin that we do not want to do.

REFLECT

I cannot skill of these thy/my ways.

Have you ever found yourself feeling confused, and thinking that God is being very unfair, when he doesn't relate to you or deal with you as you want or expect?

Richard Sibbes, one of the most important and beloved preachers in Herbert's time, and someone with whom Herbert has many affinities, speaks of how God often works by "contraries." By that he means ways that seem contradictory to us—the opposite of what makes sense to us, and would seem to us to be best.[4] This is a pattern in everyone's life with God, and part of how God is at work in us for our good and our growth in Christ-likeness, even if we do not fully understand how or why at the time.

But . . . it is also true that the reasons for our oscillating experiences of God are not always entirely mysterious. While we can be quick to question the justice of God's dealings with us when we do not like what he is doing, we are often much slower to examine the many "contraries" and contradictions in how we relate to him. In the second stanza, Herbert admits to being all over the place in his relationship with God, and that there is justice in the range of ways that God responds to him ("Thy justice me most fitly pays").

Our relationship with God is a genuine one. It should be no surprise that we sometimes experience God's rebuke as well as his affirmation. Any significant and healthy human relationship holds open the possibility of pushback when we say or do something hurtful, inappropriate, or wrong. This is uncomfortable, but we also know that the other person wouldn't bother to say anything if we and our relationship didn't matter to them.

This is even more true of our relationship with God, who alone both fully knows and fully loves us, and whose every response to us is for our good. Notice how, in the first stanza, those responses that Herbert feels as negative do not have the first word (the first word is that God has made us) and do not have the last word either. God relieving and reprieving us is the trajectory of all his ways with us.

Even so, we need to be very, very careful here. God is not a slot machine, as if when we do x or y, his automatic response will be a or b. Also, the biblical concept of God rebuking those whom he loves has been terribly

4. Sibbes draws on this theme in several places, most famously in ch. 22 of his *The Bruised Reed*, in *Selected Works*, 84–88.

abused within very human and very flawed pastoral and personal relationships. It is no wonder that many of us are even more reluctant than Herbert is here to accept the validity of what we perceive as God's "negative" responses to us. Many of us are also on very high alert for language that even hints at abusive patterns in relationships. Aspects of this poem might well be troubling to us today.

And yet . . . this poem reminds us of a profound and important truth: we are in a genuinely living, loving, responsive relationship with God. That includes being able to be honest with God in expressing our confusion and disappointment with him. It also includes recognizing that God might well push back on us for the ways in which we fall short in our side of the relationship. If so, any no we hear from God will always be in the service of his greater yes to us becoming more fully who we are called to be in him.

SCRIPTURE: EZEKIEL 18:29–32

DWELL

- Which words, images, or phrases from the poem stand out to you? Ask the Holy Spirit to speak to you through them.
- What thoughts, feelings, or actions are prompted in you as you bring the poem and the Scripture text into conversation with each other? Hold these promptings before God.
- Has God dealt with you in ways that have confused you? Be honest in expressing this, and the feelings that arise in you, to God in prayer.
- Ask the Holy Spirit to help you to be as specific as Herbert about some of the ways that you are as all over the place as he is in your own relationship with God.
- Our experience of healthy or unhealthy human relationships, especially in terms of giving and receiving criticism, will greatly affect how we respond to this poem. Reflect on the ways that this is true for you. Ask the Holy Spirit to lead you toward healing if that is needed, and to help you to entrust yourself to the loving faithfulness of God.

PRAY

> O Lord, you know, understand, and desire the good of my soul. Wretch that I am, I can neither know, nor understand, nor desire that as I ought. O Lord, out of your ineffably great love, I beseech you to do in, with, and for me whatever is most pleasing to you, and best for me. Amen.[5]

GOING FORWARD

Notice—and give thanks for—the work that God has been doing in you through this poem. Be attentive to any next steps God might be inviting you to take.

5. For this prayer I have adapted the commendation in Tuesday's daily prayers in Andrewes, *Preces Privatae*, 69. The older language in the translation by F. E. Brightman makes the connection with Herbert's poem even clearer: "O Lord, Thou knowest and canst skill and willest the good of my soul: wretched man that I am, I neither know, neither can skill, neither (as I ought) will it."

Prayer (II)

One of the many ways that Herbert can mentor us is in teaching us how to pray, and how to be honest about our varied experiences of prayer. As we've seen, Herbert sometimes wrestles with God in prayer, sometimes he wheedles, other times he doubts whether God is even listening at all, but he prays anyway. He knows that beneath all of his changeable feelings is the assurance he offers to us here, in one of his most serenely confident poems.

Of what an easy quick access,
My blessèd Lord, art thou! How suddenly
May our requests thine ear invade!
To show that state dislikes not easiness,[1]
If I but lift mine eyes, my suit is made:[2]
Thou canst no more not hear, than thou canst die.

Of what supreme almighty power
Is thy great arm, which spans the east and west,
And tacks the centre to the sphere![3]
By it do all things live their measur'd hour:
We cannot ask the thing which is not there,
Blaming the shallowness of our request.[4]

1. "State" means majesty; "easiness" signifies informality, ease of access.

2. "My suit is made" means my petition is heard.

3. We might paraphrase this line today as "keeps the earth attached to the solar system."

4. There is nothing we can ask for over which God is not already sovereign, calling into question the shallowness of our prayers.

Of what unmeasurable love
Art thou posses'd, who, when thou couldst not die,
Wert fain to take our flesh and curse,[5]
And for our sakes in person sin reprove,
That by destroying that which tied thy purse,
Thou mightst make way for liberality![6]

Since then these three wait on thy throne,[7]
Ease, *Power*, and *Love*; I value prayer so,
That were I to leave all but one,[8]
Wealth, fame, endowments, virtues, all should go;[9]
I and dear prayer would together dwell,
And quickly gain, for each inch lost, an ell.[10]

REFLECT

Of what an easy quick access,
My blessèd Lord, art thou!

Do you tend to overthink when it comes to prayer? What am I doing when I pray? How should I pray? Why should I pray? What does it mean to say that God listens to and answers prayer?

Or do you sometimes make prayer too complicated, experimenting with one method of prayer after another, as if you needed to find exactly the right words or ways of praying to meet with a hearing from God?

If so, Herbert's three "big ideas" in this poem might help.

First, prayer really does give us immediate access to God. "Ease" here signifies intimacy, and the implied contrast is between how easy it is for us to approach God versus how hard it is to come into the presence of an earthly king. Herbert knew the courts of two kings—James I and Charles I—and he knew how difficult it was for people to get a hearing. Not so with God. Yes, he is the infinite, eternal Lord of all, but that doesn't mean that

5. "Fain" means willing.

6. Now that sin has been destroyed, the "purse" of God's love has been opened for him to lavish his love upon us.

7. The image here is of Ease, Power, and Love as attendants at God's throne.

8. If I were to give up all (the good things in the next line) except one.

9. "Endowments" means our gifts/capacities/abilities.

10. An ell is an arm's length.

he is too high and mighty for us to approach him. We have only to look up, and the prayer of our heart is heard.

Second, the loving arms and sovereign care of the almighty Creator embrace all things and all circumstances. Nothing lies outside God's reach, which means we can take anything and everything to God in prayer.

Finally, because of Christ we can never doubt God's love toward us. Herbert probably has Romans 8:3 in mind in the third stanza, which speaks of how God sent his Son to take on our flesh and deal with sin in person. Sin is no longer a barrier to God lavishing the fullness of his love upon us. As Romans 3:25–26 tells us, the death of Christ both shows us God's just judgment upon sin and also enables God to justify sinners. Our sin (which tied God's purse strings, so to speak) has been done away with, opening the way for us to experience the overflowing liberality of his saving love.

Herbert is rarely as assured as this in his prayer-poems, and we might not always be as confident of these truths in our prayer lives either. There is one kind of gift in his honesty about his struggles, and another in presenting us with these foundational truths to hold onto. I think of this as a kind of "anchor" poem. No matter how stormy things might get, and no matter how turbulent our experiences of prayer might be, the anchor of these truths still holds. We can trust that we are always heard, and we can trust that God is never other than almighty and all-loving toward us. Whatever else we might *like* to know about prayer, this is all we *need* to know.

SCRIPTURE: MATTHEW 7:7–8

DWELL

- Which words, images, or phrases from the poem stand out to you? Ask the Holy Spirit to speak to you through them.
- What thoughts, feelings, or actions are prompted in you as you bring the poem and the Scripture text into conversation with each other? Hold these promptings before God.
- We have reflected on a wide range of poems that are either about prayer or are actual prayers—or, like this one, are both of those at once. Have you found yourself resonating more with poems like this one, where Herbert is assured and confident, or with poems where he is wrestling and struggling with God in prayer? What might you learn from this about your own prayer life?

- Which of these themes—God's "easy quick access," his "almighty power," and his "unmeasurable love"—do you find easiest to keep hold of in your prayers, and which can be more challenging for you? Has this been different at various times in your life?
- At the close, Herbert effectively says that if need be, he would give up everything and just keep hold of prayer. How does this shift your understanding of the importance of prayer? What might it mean for you to value prayer more highly?

PRAY

> Almighty and everlasting God, who art always more ready to hear than we to pray, and art wont to give more than either we desire or deserve: Pour down upon us the abundance of thy mercy; forgiving us those things whereof our conscience is afraid, and giving us those good things which we are not worthy to ask but through the merits and mediation of Jesus Christ, thy Son, our Lord. Amen.[11]

GOING FORWARD

Notice—and give thanks for—the work that God has been doing in you through this poem. Be attentive to any next steps God might be inviting you to take.

11. This is the collect for the twelfth Sunday after Trinity in the 1662 BCP.

Conscience

There's a saying that defines "Puritanism" as the fear that someone somewhere might be happy. That is *very* unfair to seventeenth-century "Puritans"! Even so, there really is such a thing an overscrupulous, hyper-legalistic conscience. Herbert reminds us here that to be a Christian does not mean being so afraid of doing something wrong that we lose all enjoyment in the legitimate delights God has given us. We can look to what Christ has done for us on the cross, not to render us complacent but to set us free from nagging fears.

Peace prattler, do not lower:[1]
Not a fair look, but thou dost call it foul:
Not a sweet dish, but thou dost call it sour:
Music to thee doth howl.
By list'ning to thy chatting fears
I have both lost mine eyes and ears.

Prattler, no more, I say:
My thoughts must work, but like a noiseless sphere;
Harmonious peace must rock them all the day:
No room for prattlers there.
If thou persistest, I will tell thee,
That I have physic to expel thee.[2]

1. To prattle is to talk foolishly nonstop; "lower" (rhymes with "sour") means to look gloomy and threatening.

2. "Physic" means medicine to purge (expel) the nagging conscience.

And the receit[3] shall be
My Saviour's blood: whenever at his board[4]
I do but taste it, straight it cleanseth me,
And leaves thee not a word,
No, not a tooth or nail to scratch,
And at my actions carp or catch.

Yet if thou talkest still,
Besides my physic, know there's some for thee:
Some wood and nails to make a staff or bill[5]
For those that trouble me:
The bloody cross of my dear Lord
Is both my physic and my sword.

REFLECT

Not a fair look, but thou dost call it foul

Do you find yourself worrying that if you are enjoying something too much it must be sinful? If you are pleased when someone compliments you, is that wicked pride? Do you feel as though you constantly have to be on your guard because "Jesus is watching you," just waiting for you to mess up so that he can come down on you like a ton of bricks?

Welcome to the world of an overactive inner critic combined with a hyper-legalistic conscience. Herbert seems to have understood it well. If all of this feels very familiar to you, I hope you are cheering inside right now! In this poem, Herbert silences his prattling, carping, overzealous conscience with a gospel dressing down. No, we do *not* need to be living in constant fear of tripping up—the kind of fear that can prevent us from doing perfectly acceptable things, or which can poison the legitimate delight that comes from enjoying God's good gifts. No, Jesus is *not* waiting to pounce on us for the slightest slip. It is because of Jesus, says Herbert, that we have been set free from such niggling fears.

There's a danger here, of course, and Herbert is well aware of it. We can abuse good things in ways that harm ourselves and others. We can abuse the gospel itself, by treating the saving work of Christ as permission to do

3. "Receipt" in Herbert's time meant recipe.

4. "Board" is a dining table—here the communion table.

5. These are both weapons. A staff is a large wooden stick, and a bill is a halberd—a wooden shaft topped with an axe blade and spike.

whatever we want because "my Saviour's blood . . . cleanseth me." Herbert almost certainly has 1 John 1:7 in mind here, which tells us that Christ's blood cleanses us from all sin. As the verses around that text remind us, though, this is not an excuse for willful sin, but an encouragement to all of us who are earnestly seeking to live in the light of the gospel, while also recognizing that we will still sin and fall short (1 John 1:5–10).

It is in this spirit that Herbert points us to our union with Christ and our participation in his saving work. This is the medicine the Lord's Supper holds out to us. If that isn't enough to overcome our hypercritical thoughts, though, and in an unusually violent image for the mostly very gentle Herbert, the cross can even become a holy weapon to beat them back. While Herbert will never be one to excuse our sin, it seems as though he knows full well how hard it can be for those of us who are prone to beating ourselves up to silence our inner critic.

SCRIPTURE: 1 CORINTHIANS 10:31

DWELL

- Which words, images, or phrases from the poem stand out to you? Ask the Holy Spirit to speak to you through them.
- What thoughts, feelings, or actions are prompted in you as you bring the poem and the Scripture text into conversation with each other? Hold these promptings before God.
- In this poem, Herbert's conscience is objecting to the enjoyment he takes in what he sees, hears, and tastes. What good gifts of God does your inner critic try to poison for you?
- Notice that the criticisms of Herbert's "prattling" conscience are driven by fear. Take some time to reflect on how this might be true for you as well. How might Herbert's appeal to the saving work of Christ help you in that regard?
- It's all very well not to want our thoughts to be disturbed by an overzealous conscience, but sometimes we do need to be jolted out of our complacency. How do you discern between the unhealthy nagging of your inner critic and the needful work of the Holy Spirit to help you recognize important ways that you are falling short?

PRAY

Lord Jesus,
you came that we might have life,
and have it abundantly.
You enjoyed food and drink with friends so much
that your critics called you a glutton and a drunkard.
You supplied gallons of fine wine at a wedding.
You honored the extravagant gift of perfume poured out,
so that the scent filled the whole house.
Sanctify our senses so that we can taste and see
And hear and touch and smell that you are good.
All good things come to us through you.
May we receive them gratefully,
rightly honoring your gifts
by delighting in them and using them well,
to your praise and glory. Amen.[6]

GOING FORWARD

Notice—and give thanks for—the work that God has been doing in you through this poem. Be attentive to any next steps God might be inviting you to take.

6. I wrote this prayer as part of my response to "Conscience" when I journaled my way through Herbert's poetry.

The Dawning

This is a very different kind of Easter poem from the joyful one we reflected on earlier. Here is a poem for all of us who have found ourselves weeping when everyone else is rejoicing.

Awake sad heart, whom sorrow ever drowns;
    Take up thine eyes, which feed on earth;
Unfold thy forehead gather'd into frowns:
    Thy Saviour comes, and with him mirth:[1]
                        Awake, awake;
And with a thankful heart his comforts take.
    But thou dost still lament, and pine, and cry;[2]
    And feel his death, but not his victory.

Arise sad heart; if thou dost not withstand,
    Christ's resurrection thine may be:
Do not by hanging down break from the hand,
    Which as it riseth, raiseth thee:
                        Arise, arise;
And with his burial-linen dry thine eyes:
    Christ left his grave-clothes, that we might, when grief
    Draws tears, or blood, not want an handkerchief.[3]

1. "Mirth" in Herbert's time signified joy, not merely mild amusement.
2. "Still" means always.
3. "Want" means lack.

REFLECT

But thou dost still lament . . .
And feel [Christ's] death, but not his victory.

Have there been times in your life when you simply haven't been able to join in the rejoicing at Easter (or Christmas, or other times of celebration)? Some of us might be grieving. Others of us might be dealing with a difficult diagnosis, or perhaps there's something seriously amiss at home or at work. Maybe we are trudging our way through a season of illness or depression. Whatever the reasons, we just aren't "feeling it." Perhaps we even avoid worship because we can't face the disjunct between the celebratory mood and what we are dealing with in our lives.

Herbert has been there. He knows what it is like to feel as though you are drowning in sorrow when everyone else is singing. Since this is an Easter poem, he describes it as like being stuck in mourning for Christ's death, unable to experience the joy of his victorious resurrection.

In many ways, this is a companion piece to our earlier Easter poem. That one is exuberantly joyful, and begins with Herbert exhorting his heart to rise and sing. All he can manage here is to summon his heart to wake up from its numbness and at least look up from its sorrow to see the risen Christ. As many of us know, when we are struggling it can feel as though we are dragging ourselves from one thing to the next. We often find ourselves with our heads down, literally looking at the ground, and also looking downward into ourselves. It is hard not to be almost entirely absorbed in what is troubling us. Herbert's gentle hint to look up—physically and spiritually—is well taken.

Even if we cannot share in the full-on joy and celebration, Herbert doesn't want us to miss out on the loving comfort that is still ours in the Lord. He returns to the most beautiful, intimate image from his earlier Easter poem, and his favorite way of depicting Christ's tender love for us, which we will see in several more poems: Christ taking our hand. Christ is doing all heavy lifting here, so to speak, even when we are very heavy indeed. We do not need to do anything. The best we can muster is not to withstand Christ, and to keep hold of his hand as he raises us up with him.

Herbert is also echoing the Song of Songs 2:10–13 in his exhortation to his heart to arise. In those verses, the lover (interpreted as Christ) tells the beloved (the Christian) how beautiful she is and urges her to arise and come away with him. Herbert is gently reminding us that even when we are struggling and downcast, we are still beloved.

The reality beyond our circumstances is that Christ is risen, even if we barely notice it, and he has won the victory for us, even if we cannot feel it. Even if it seems as though you are stuck at the tomb while everyone else is celebrating the risen Lord, he still has something there for you. The burial linen he left behind (John 20:5–7) is to wipe away your tears. But the hope of this poem is that, like Mary Magdalen grieving at the tomb early on that first Easter morning, there will be the dawning realization that the risen Lord is with you.

SCRIPTURE: JOHN 20:11–18

DWELL

- Which words, images, or phrases from the poem stand out to you? Ask the Holy Spirit to speak to you through them.
- What thoughts, feelings, or actions are prompted in you as you bring the poem and the Scripture text into conversation with each other? Hold these promptings before God.
- Sometimes it can feel as though being happy—or at least, pretending to be happy—is a requirement when it comes to the public face of being a Christian. Have you felt the pressure to hide your sadness or your struggles? How might we do better at making room for acknowledging when things are not OK, and at supporting each other along the way?
- When you are feeling downcast, how might you remind yourself to take on board Herbert's gentle encouragement to look upward and outward to Christ?
- Think back to a time when you felt weighed down with sorrow and trouble—or perhaps you are feeling like that now. Where do you find Christ's comfort most in this poem? The image of him holding your hand? The recognition that he still comes to you and is present to you even when you are struggling? The reminder that you are beloved? The oddly tender image of his burial linen to wipe away your tears? Spend time simply sitting with whatever resonates most with you, and "with a thankful heart his comforts take."

PRAY

Loving Lord Jesus,
come to us in our distress, we pray.
Lift up our hearts when we are cast down.
Help us to look up and see you through our tears.
May the glorious light of your love
shine like a beacon to lead us out of our darkness.
We pray this in your name,
our crucified and risen Lord and Savior,
Amen.[4]

GOING FORWARD

Notice—and give thanks for—the work that God has been doing in you through this poem. Be attentive to any next steps God might be inviting you to take.

4. This is another prayer from my journal, as part of my response to this poem.

Dialogue

Here is a vivid and moving presentation of some of the deepest mysteries of our salvation. Aspects of theology that might seem puzzling and off putting if we merely ponder them intellectually are brought to life in a conversation between Herbert and Christ.

Sweetest Saviour, if my soul
　　Were but worth the having,
Quickly should I then control
　　Any thought of waving.[1]
But when all my care and pains
Cannot give the name of gains
To thy wretch so full of stains,
What delight or hope remains?

What, child, is the balance thine,
　　Thine the poise and measure?[2]
If I say, "Thou shalt be mine,"
　　Finger not my treasure.[3]
What the gains in having thee
Do amount to, only he
Who for man was sold can see;
That transferr'd th'accounts to me.

1. "Waving" suggests the poet both "waiving" any claims to salvation in Christ and also "wavering."

2. The main image here is of balance scales (poise, measure), but balance also points to a financial ledger for balancing the budget.

3. In other words, "Don't touch! Hands off my treasure!"

But as I can see no merit
    Leading to this favour,
So the way to fit me for it
    Is beyond my savour.[4]
As the reason, then, is thine,
So the way is none of mine;
I disclaim the whole design;
Sin disclaims and I resign.[5]

That is all, if that I could
    Get without repining;
And my clay, my creature, would
    Follow my resigning;
That as I did freely part
With my glory and desert,
Left all joys to feel all smart[6]*—*
    Ah! No more: thou break'st my heart.

REFLECT

If I say, "Thou shalt be mine,"
Finger not my treasure.

Have you sometimes felt like you are more trouble to God than you could possibly be worth?

In the opening stanza, Herbert attempts to persuade Christ to give up on him. He isn't worthy. He isn't good enough. He has tried over and over to do better, but he keeps messing up. There really isn't any point to either of them trying to keep going with this. It isn't working.

He receives the loving but rather imperious response that it is none of his business why Christ would love him and save him. That is a matter of Christ's sovereign choice and his free grace, and it is not up to Herbert to weigh up his own worth. It's not up to us either. To echo the answer to the first question of the Heidelberg Catechism ("What is your only comfort in

4. The way to fit me for it (Christ's saving love) is beyond my understanding, but perhaps with hints of not being to my taste too: "I don't get it, and I don't like it."

5. To disclaim is to repudiate. In the line above, it is Herbert who disclaims his salvation. In the last line it is "Sin." Perhaps there is just a hint here of the reversal to come. This is sin at work in Herbert, but sin does not have the last word on the matter (Romans 7:14–25).

6. "Smart" means pain.

life and in death?"), Christ is reminding Herbert and us that we are not our own. We belong entirely to our Savior, who has paid for all our sins with his precious blood.

At this point in the poem, though, this is not a comfort to Herbert. It riles him up no end. He abandons the attempt to get Christ to give up on him and instead seeks to give up on Christ. In doing that he speaks for all of us who, at one time or another, have wanted to abandon the struggle of trying to live for Christ. In effect, he says, "You're right. This really *is* your business, not mine. I haven't asked for any of this. I haven't done anything to deserve it. I don't like or understand it. I reject the whole deal. I resign."

But Christ picks up on Herbert's final words and gently outwits him. "I resign" is exactly the right response, even if not in the way that Herbert intended. We need to resign our obsession with our worth and merit (or lack of it), and our willful resistance to Christ's love. Instead, we need to surrender to grace and then learn what it means to follow the way of Christ, who resigned the glory and the joys of heaven out of love, to endure everything it would take to redeem us (Philippians 2:5–11). It is this reminder of the magnitude of Christ's self-giving love that breaks Herbert's heart, and his resistance.

This conversation presents us afresh with salvation as Christ's sovereign choice to love otherwise unlovable sinners like us, in sheer, undeserved grace. We see how that very grace is what enables us to freely surrender ourselves to the beautiful mystery of his love. And despite Herbert's attempts to cast himself off, we witness Christ's unbreakable loving hold upon his own. None can snatch us from his hand (John 10:28), and neither will he allow us to slip through his fingers.

SCRIPTURE: JOHN 10:27–30

DWELL

- Which words, images, or phrases from the poem stand out to you? Ask the Holy Spirit to speak to you through them.
- What thoughts, feelings, or actions are prompted in you as you bring the poem and the Scripture text into conversation with each other? Hold these promptings before God.
- How hard it can be sometimes to accept that we are loved by God! But the poem is correct. We are not in any position to weigh up our worth

before God. We simply are eternally treasured and infinitely beloved. Ask God to give you a fresh sense of your immeasurable worth to him.

- The kind of "resignation" that this poem teaches us is not easy. It calls us to focus less on ourselves, and what we do or don't deserve, and more on what it means to follow in the way of the self-giving love of Christ. Ask the Holy Spirit to give you more of a spirit of holy resignation.
- One of the most beautiful things about this poem is how Christ will not allow Herbert to have the last self-destructive word, but turns that around into yet more love and grace. Take time to reflect on how Christ has not let you—and will not let you—have the last hurtful word about yourself. Let that break your heart in a good way, so that you can rest secure in his love.

PRAY

Loving Lord Jesus, my only comfort is that I am not my own, but that I belong—body and soul, in life and in death—to you, my faithful Savior. You have redeemed me with your precious blood. You watch over me. You guide and govern me so that all things work together for my salvation. By your Holy Spirit assure me of eternal life, and make me wholeheartedly willing and ready from now on to live for you. Amen.[7]

GOING FORWARD

Notice—and give thanks for—the work that God has been doing in you through this poem. Be attentive to any next steps God might be inviting you to take.

7. Here I have turned the words of the Heidelberg Catechism Q&A 1 into a prayer. You can readily find the text of the catechism online.

Sin's Round

This is a poem that will leave us nodding—and squirming—because Herbert gets to the heart of how surreptitiously sin works and grows in us. "Sin's Round" is such an evocative title because this poem shows us how our sinful tendencies can go round and round in circles, and like a musical round, it can be hard to know when the sinful cycles might stop.

Sorry I am, my God, sorry I am,
That my offenses course it in a ring.[1]
My thoughts are working like a busy flame,
Until their cockatrice they hatch and bring;[2]
And when they once have perfected their draughts,[3]
My words take fire from my inflamèd thoughts.

My words take fire from my inflamèd thoughts,
Which spit it forth like the Sicilian Hill.[4]
They vent the wares, and pass them with their faults,
And by their breathing ventilate the ill.
But words suffice not, where are lewd intentions:[5]
My hands do join to finish the inventions.

1. "Course it in a ring" means dance in a circle.

2. A cockatrice is a mythical beast—part serpent, part bird—that hatched from an egg and could kill with its breath. The cockatrice mentioned in the KJV translation of Isaiah 59:4–5 is almost certainly what Herbert has in mind here.

3. "Draughts" means drafts, and also the draught hole of a furnace to let air in.

4. The Sicilian Hill is the volcano Mt. Etna.

5. In Herbert's time, "lewd intentions" didn't just imply sexual sin. It included any kind of wickedness.

My hands do join to finish the inventions:
And so my sins ascend three stories high,
As Babel grew,[6] before there were dissensions.
Yet ill deeds loiter not: for they supply
New thoughts of sinning: wherefore, to my shame,
Sorry I am, my God, sorry I am.

REFLECT

Sorry I am, my God, sorry I am.

Do you find yourself stewing over something—perhaps a person or situation, or perhaps an issue in the news or on social media? You go over and over whatever it is in your head, and your thoughts become inflamed until they lead to a fierce explosion of words. Maybe you speak them out loud. Maybe you hit send on an email, message, or post. And then words often aren't enough. Actions follow . . . which lead to more thoughts . . . and so on.

That is the vicious sin cycle of this poem. Notice how the last line of each stanza is the same as the first line of the next. This helps us to see the sneaky spiral of sin: inflamed thoughts lead to volcanic words; words give oxygen to what fired us up in the first place, leading to harmful actions; and then our deeds lead back to more sinful thoughts, and so the whole cycle begins again.

That is why Herbert begins and ends this poem with the same words, "Sorry I am, my God, sorry I am." That is the big-picture cycle of sin and repentance in our lives right there. Every day, in all sorts of ways, we fall short of how we should live before God and toward others, and so we need to keep going before God to acknowledge that we have messed up, and that we are sorry.

This poem's painfully insightful account of sin is rooted in a prayer of confession from the 1662 BCP communion service: "We acknowledge and bewail our manifold sins and wickedness, which we . . . have committed by thought, word, and deed. . . . We do earnestly repent, and are heartily sorry for these our misdoings."

Herbert could also depend upon his first readers knowing what came next in the service. On its own, this poem appears bleak, with its seemingly endless cycle of falling short and having to say sorry. But always in worship,

6. The tower of Babel (Genesis 11:1–9).

after a prayer of confession, comes the absolution, which speaks of God's forgiveness, and of us being enabled and strengthened to live more fully toward him. As you dwell with this poem, keep that in mind too. Yes, you will need to keep on saying sorry to God for what you have done amiss in thought, word, and deed. But there is forgiveness in Christ, and the ongoing, transforming work of the Holy Spirit.

SCRIPTURE: 1 JOHN 1:8–9

DWELL

- Which words, images, or phrases from the poem stand out to you? Ask the Holy Spirit to speak to you through them.
- What thoughts, feelings, or actions are prompted in you as you bring the poem and the Scripture text into conversation with each other? Hold these promptings before God.
- Are there people, issues, or situations that tend to inflame your thoughts and lead you to explosive words, spoken or written? Ask the Holy Spirit to channel these thoughts toward more constructive words and deeds.
- Do you find that your thoughts tend to drift toward something you know is wrong, and then you find yourself justifying it, and then doing whatever that thing is . . . again? Pray for your thoughts to be directed toward whatever is true, noble, pure, and admirable (Philippians 4:8), and don't hesitate to seek help if you feel as though you are trapped in an addictive spiral that is hurtful to yourself and others.
- Be intentional and honest in looking back over the past few days and holding before Christ the ways you have fallen short of who you are called to be in him. But also remember that confession and repentance open the way to receiving the triune God's forgiveness and a fresh start.

PRAY

Almighty God, our heavenly Father,
we have sinned against you
and against our neighbour

in thought and word and deed,
through negligence, through weakness,
through our own deliberate fault.
We are truly sorry
and repent of all our sins.
For the sake of your Son Jesus Christ,
who died for us,
forgive us all that is past
and grant that we may serve you in newness of life
to the glory of your name.
Amen.[7]

GOING FORWARD

Notice—and give thanks for—the work that God has been doing in you through this poem. Be attentive to any next steps God might be inviting you to take.

7. This is a prayer of confession from Holy Communion Order One in the Church of England's *Common Worship*, 169.

Gratefulness

Here is a prayer-poem that is intimate and wise, fun and serious, full of wry, self-aware humor and love. May we all find ourselves so comfortable in God's presence that we can pray like this too!

Thou that hast giv'n so much to me,
Give one thing more, a grateful heart.
See how thy beggar works on thee
By art.

He makes thy gifts occasion more,[1]
And says, If he in this be cross'd
All thou hast giv'n him heretofore
Is lost.[2]

But thou didst reckon,[3] when at first
Thy word our hearts and hands did crave,[4]
What it would come to at the worst
To save.

1. "Occasion more" means give rise to more.

2. If God refuses this request, all his other gifts will have been wasted.

3. "Reckon" is an accounting term tht means to tally up or calculate.

4. This is a very sneaky line! My first instinct when I read it is always to interpret it as "when our hearts and hands first desired God's word." But it could *also* mean when *Christ* (the Word of God) first desired *our* hearts and hands (in other words, our love and service). Very possibly Herbert intends both of those meanings!

Perpetual knockings at thy door,[5]
Tears sullying thy transparent rooms,
Gift upon gift, much would have more,
And comes.[6]

This notwithstanding, thou went'st on,
And didst allow us all our noise:
Nay thou hast made a sigh and groan
Thy joys.

Not that thou hast not still above
Much better tunes than groans can make;
But that these country airs thy love
Did take.[7]

Wherefore I cry and cry again;
And in no quiet canst thou be,
Till I a thankful heart obtain
Of thee:

Not thankful when it pleaseth me,
As if thy blessings had spare days[8]
But such a heart whose pulse may be
Thy praise.

REFLECT

Thou that hast giv'n so much to me,
Give one thing more, a grateful heart.

Herbert is right, isn't he? We are always asking God for things, and God really has given so much to us. Yet most of the time we hardly even acknowledge that, and sometimes we don't even notice, let alone give thanks.

What's more, we can't *make* ourselves be grateful. Think of a child being told to say thank you to a relative who has given them a present they don't particularly like. If we are obliged to show gratitude when we don't

5. E.g., Matthew 7:7–8, where Jesus tells his disciples to ask, seek, and knock.

6. The one who receives much wants more, and comes to get it.

7. "Country airs" are uncouth rustic tunes (vs. courtly music)—but God has taken to loving them.

8. As if God took days off from blessing us.

really feel it, the best we can come up with is an inwardly grudging outward expression of thanks. True gratitude, though, simply wells up from within us. Sadly, because of the impact of sin, we even need to ask God to give us the very thing that should be most natural to us: a grateful heart in response to who God is and what God has done.

But God knows what he got himself into by loving people like us. Herbert hints at a scenario from his own time to get the message across. It is as if God in heaven with his angels and saints is like a lord in his splendid manor house. He keeps noble, sophisticated company there, and enjoys fine music, but scruffy, unruly beggars keep turning up at the door to pester him. Somehow, though, he doesn't seem to mind. He even seems to rather like them. They are ragged and dirty, and make a mess of his nice, clean rooms. They are endlessly asking for things, and always wanting more, with cries and pleas and sighs and groans which make for embarrassingly awful "music"—like clumsily played rustic tunes in comparison to the polished, sophisticated, courtly music more fitting for a noble lord. But this Lord delights to welcome these beggars and to keep on giving them what they need. And the uncouth sound of their cries and pleas is somehow as beautiful to him as glorious heavenly music.

And so Herbert comes back yet again, to plead for that one thing more. When I read the second last stanza, I can't help but think of the Christmas song "We Wish You a Merry Christmas." I expect most of us know the first stanza, but do you know the next two? "Now bring us some figgy pudding . . . Now bring some right here" and then "We won't go until we get some . . . So bring some out here!" Now give me a grateful heart, Lord. And I won't go until I get one, so bring it right here!

Never a day goes by when there isn't something for which to thank God. What we need—and long for—is a heart that is grateful not just when we feel like it, but whose every beat is gratitude: "such a heart whose pulse may be / Thy praise."

SCRIPTURE: 1 THESSALONIANS 5:16–18

DWELL

- Which words, images, or phrases from the poem stand out to you? Ask the Holy Spirit to speak to you through them.

- What thoughts, feelings, or actions are prompted in you as you bring the poem and the Scripture text into conversation with each other? Hold these promptings before God.
- There is something wonderfully freeing about the reminder that God doesn't despise (or even merely tolerate) our endless, noisy, mixed-up prayers. He delights in them. Our messy prayers are welcome. What difference might this assurance make to how you pray?
- What might it mean for gratitude to God to be like the heartbeat of your life? While we cannot manufacture it, we can cultivate practices that attune our hearts to thankfulness. Perhaps we could be intentional about beginning our prayer times with praise and thanksgiving, rather than rushing straight to requests. Perhaps at the end of the day or the week we could reflect back on causes for thanksgiving. Perhaps we could make a list of blessings and answered prayers at key moments in our lives and offer our thanks to God for them.
- Herbert says that God doesn't take days off when it comes to giving us reasons for thanksgiving. If we're honest, though, it sometimes doesn't feel like that. There can be whole seasons in our lives when we struggle to see God's blessings, and when our prayers are filled with requests that God doesn't seem to be answering. Ask the Holy Spirit to show you how you might still give thanks, bearing in mind that we are exhorted to give thanks *in* all circumstances, not necessarily *for* those circumstances.

PRAY

Almighty God, we give you thanks
for this life and all its blessings,
for joys great and simple,
for gifts and powers more than we deserve,
for love at the heart of your purpose
and surpassing wisdom in all your works,
for light in the world
brought once in Jesus Christ
and shining ever through his Spirit.

We pray, through Jesus Christ our Lord,
for that light to dawn upon us daily,
that we may always have a grateful heart,
and a will to love and serve you
to the end of our days.
Amen.[9]

GOING FORWARD

Notice—and give thanks for—the work that God has been doing in you through this poem. Be attentive to any next steps God might be inviting you to take.

9. Thanksgiving 2 from "Additional Prayers for Public Worship," in the Church of Scotland's *Book of Common Order*, 498.

The Storm

In some ways, this is one aspect of our previous poem in action, as Herbert envisages a storm of sighs and tears battering heaven's doors, and drowning out the heavenly music. And Herbert is right, isn't he? Sometimes we need a good storm to clear the air.

If as the winds and waters here below
                    Do fly and flow,
My sighs and tears as busy were above;
                    Sure they would move
And much affect thee, as tempestuous times
Amaze poor mortals, and object their crimes.[1]

Stars have their storms, ev'n in a high degree,[2]
                    As well as we.
A throbbing conscience spurred by remorse
                    Hath a strange force:
It quits the earth, and mounting more and more
Dares to assault thee, and besiege thy door.[3]

1. "Object their crimes" (the accent is on the second syllable) means make them aware of their crimes or accuse them of their crimes. In Herbert's time, stormy weather was sometimes interpreted as an indication of something amiss in society that required collective repentance.

2. Astronomical events such as meteor showers were seen as the result of storms among the stars.

3. The storm metaphor shifts here from the weather to the other main meaning of the word in the seventeenth century: besiegers launching an attack on a castle or city.

There it stands knocking,[4] to thy music's wrong,
And drowns the song.
Glory and honour are set by, till it
An answer get.[5]
Poets have wrong'd poor storms: such days are best.
They purge the air without, within the breast.

REFLECT

Such days are best.
They purge the air without, within the breast.

As it is with the weather, so it is in our lives. We might try to suppress whatever it is that is troubling us, but the pressure builds and builds until eventually a storm erupts. Sometimes that is the opposite of helpful, like when we explode with rage against someone. At other times, though, it is exactly what we need, such as when we finally allow ourselves to release all of our pent-up emotions in a flood of tears.

As Herbert knows full well, we often try any number of strategies to avoid acknowledging to ourselves, let alone to God, how we have fallen short of God's ways. We do that even though we also know what a sheer relief it is to finally be open and honest, and to pour everything out to God in confession. Our Scripture text will remind us of that as well.

In some ways this is a companion piece to the poem "Conscience," which we reflected on earlier. There, Herbert was rightly keeping his over-scrupulous conscience in check. Here, he is describing how our conscience ought to work: throbbing with remorse and giving us no peace until we stop trying to hide, excuse, or repress where we have gone wrong, and the storm bursts as we bring it all to God in heartfelt sorrow and penitence.

Herbert is right. Such days are best. God welcomes the interruption, so to speak, and such storms clear the air with God, as we seek both his forgiveness and his purging, transforming work in us.

4. This is an echo of Jesus' words about prayer: Knock and the door will be opened to you (Matthew 7:8).

5. There is rich ambiguity here. Does this mean that God sets aside his glory and honor to answer the conscience, or does it signify that the conscience has set aside praising and glorifying God while it besieges God for an answer to its troubles?

SCRIPTURE: PSALM 32:1–7

DWELL

- Which words, images, or phrases from the poem stand out to you? Ask the Holy Spirit to speak to you through them.
- What thoughts, feelings, or actions are prompted in you as you bring the poem and the Scripture text into conversation with each other? Hold these promptings before God.
- Think back to a time when you tried to suppress your conscience. Did the storm eventually break into repentance and confession? Ask the Holy Spirit to help you to probe how and why you resist being honest with yourself and with God about where you have gone wrong.
- Herbert is envisaging a helpful storm here, in which remorse for how we have failed to walk in God's ways bursts out and clears the air. Have there been good and not-so-good storms in your relationship with God and with others? Listen for what the Lord might have to teach you as you reflect on those experiences.
- Herbert assures us in this poem that God is eager to hear and answer us when we turn to him with our sorrow for sin. This is reminiscent of Jesus telling us that there is great rejoicing in heaven when someone repents (Luke 15:7,10). Allow these thoughts to dispel any fear or reluctance that you might have when it comes to bringing everything about yourself to God.

PRAY

> Grant, we beseech thee, merciful Lord, to thy faithful people pardon and peace; that they may be cleansed from all their sins and serve thee with a quiet mind; through Jesus Christ our Lord. Amen.[6]

GOING FORWARD

Notice—and give thanks for—the work that God has been doing in you through this poem. Be attentive to any next steps God might be inviting you to take.

6. This is the collect for the twenty-first Sunday after Trinity in the 1662 BCP.

Artillery

Here is an imaginative story-poem that shows how Herbert can be witty and bold, lighthearted and poignant all at once in his relationship with God. So can we.

As I one evening sat before my cell,[1]
Me thoughts a star did shoot into my lap.[2]
I rose and shook my clothes, as knowing well
That from small fires comes oft no small mishap;
    When suddenly I heard one say:
    Do as thou usest, disobey,
    Expel good motions from thy breast,
Which have the face of fire, but end in rest.[3]

I, who had heard of music in the spheres,[4]
But not of speech in stars, began to muse;
But turning to my God, whose ministers
The stars and all things are: "If I refuse,
    Dread Lord," said I, "so oft my good,
    Then I refuse not ev'n with blood[5]
    To wash away my stubborn thought;
For I will do or suffer what I ought.

1. A "cell" is the lodging of a hermit or monk.

2. "Me thoughts" means I thought/it seemed to me.

3. "Do as thou usest" means do as you always do; "motions" means promptings; "have the face of fire" means that outwardly they seem dangerous.

4. The music of the spheres is the Pythagorean idea that the movement of the stars and planets is a form of music, creating perfect mathematical harmonies.

5. This is a classically ambiguous moment from Herbert. Whose blood will wash away his stubborn thoughts? Christ's redeeming blood, most certainly, but is it his own as well, implying his willingness to suffer the consequences of his resistance to God's promptings?

But I have also stars and shooters too,
Born where thy servants both artilleries use.
My tears and prayers night and day do woo
And work up to thee; yet thou dost refuse.
  Not but I am (I must say still)[6]
  Much more oblig'd to do thy will
  Than thou to grant mine; but because
Thy promise now hath ev'n set thee thy laws.

Then we are shooters both, and thou dost deign
To enter combat with us, and contest
With thine own clay.[7] But I would parley fain:[8]
Shun not my arrows, and behold my breast.
  Yet if thou shunnest, I am thine:
  I must be so, if I am mine.
  There is no articling with thee:[9]
I am but finite, yet thine infinitely."

REFLECT

Then we are shooters both

We've all done it, haven't we? We've tried to dismiss a prompting from the Holy Spirit because it challenged us too much, threatening to disrupt the usual cautious, comfortable ways we live our lives.

Herbert has a priceless story and image for that here! He imagines a shooting star landing in his lap, so he leaps up to dash it off in case the sparks set his clothes on fire. And then he hears a voice saying, in effect, "Here you go again! Disobedient as always! Trying to push away a holy prompting because it freaked you out, when actually it's the way for you to find true peace."

But then Herbert turns the tables! He is prepared to repent and take the consequences for all the times that he has disobeyed God's "good motions,"

6. "Not but" means not so much that.

7. The reference to clay here echoes God's creation of Adam in Genesis 2:7, and also the image found in Isaiah and Jeremiah of God as the potter and us as clay.

8. "I would parley fain" means I would like to seek a truce.

9. "No articling" with God is an incredibly rich phrase! It means that there is no bringing a legal charge against God, no winning an argument with God, and no coming to articles of agreement for a surrender.

but he points out that if he brushes off promptings from God, God seems to be brushing off his prayers too. For Herbert, as for the Psalms, prayer is not for the mealy mouthed or fainthearted. Are you prepared to be as audacious as Herbert in your conversations with God?

Herbert is the perfect blend of boldness and realistic humility here. He acknowledges that God is God and he is not, so he is much more obliged to do God's will than God is to do his. He also recognizes that even if God chooses to ignore him ("if thou shunnest") he still belongs to God ("I am thine: / I must be so, if I am mine"). (Later we will see Herbert tying himself in playful knots with wordplay on thine/mine in his poem "Clasping of Hands.") Even so, he is prepared to push back. God has bound himself to promises, and it feels to Herbert like God is going back on them. So Herbert and God are "shooters both." God is shooting his "good motions" at Herbert to show him how to walk in his ways. Herbert is firing tears and prayers back at God, to try to get God to do what he wants.

This is a battle of love. Herbert draws on images from love poetry, where lovers both fire and surrender themselves to the dart of love ("Shun not my arrows, and behold my breast"). In turn this language was regularly co-opted into the realm of our relationship with God. In Herbert's time there were many actual and poetic images of the arrow of divine love piercing human hearts, as well as prayer arrows rising to God.

As a finite creature tackling the infinite God, this is also an impossibly unequal fight, and yet God deigns to enter into combat with us on our terms. Like the angel who wrestles with Jacob, God could completely overwhelm us if he chose, but Herbert knows that God is not that kind of God. God wants us to be up front with him, calling us into a genuine and robust relationship with himself. That means he is prepared to wrestle with us as we wrestle with him.

In the process, we learn more about God and ourselves, and our relationship with God is all the stronger for it. And in this battle of love there is no ceasefire. God will always be shooting the promptings of his "good motions" at us, and we will always be shooting the arrows of our prayers to him. This will be a lifelong exchange of loving artillery—or, to shift the metaphor, a lifelong wrestling match with God, which is also a loving embrace.

SCRIPTURE: GENESIS 32:24–30

DWELL

- Which words, images, or phrases from the poem stand out to you? Ask the Holy Spirit to speak to you through them.
- What thoughts, feelings, or actions are prompted in you as you bring the poem and the Scripture text into conversation with each other? Hold these promptings before God.
- Can you recall a time when you instinctively rejected what turned out to be a prompting from the Holy Spirit? Why was that? Did it challenge you too deeply, or seem too risky, or . . . ? Join Herbert in acknowledging when you have shaken off "good motions" from God.
- What makes you "fire back" toward God? Or do you struggle with the idea of speaking back to God? What do you find encouraging or difficult about Herbert's combination of boldness and humility in this poem?
- What difference does it make to situate the give-and-take in your relationship with God within the reality that you are infinitely his?

PRAY

Almighty, holy, loving God,
sometimes it feels as though we are in combat with you, and you with us.
You challenge us to contest with you,
and yet as we wrestle with you and pray to you, we know that it is you who give us the weapons and the strength for the struggle.
We also know that even as you fight against us when we go wrong,
at the same time, you are also fighting for us, to set us right.
Sustain us in this holy combat.
Enable us to overcome all that would lead us away from you
and grant us your blessing we pray.
Amen.[10]

10. I wrote this prayer based on Calvin's commentary on Genesis 32, in which he interprets Jacob wrestling with the angel in terms of a trial of faith, to see if we will keep hold of God in the midst of temptation.

GOING FORWARD

Notice—and give thanks for—the work that God has been doing in you through this poem. Be attentive to any next steps God might be inviting you to take.

The Holdfast

We like to say that everything about our salvation is a gift of God's grace, but as this poem makes clear, the full implications of that might leave us feeling perplexed and uncomfortable. With wonderful lightness of touch Herbert gives us a theology lesson here, and it has significant implications for our faith lives.

I threatened to observe the strict decree
        Of my dear God with all my power & might.
        But I was told by one, it could not be;
Yet I might trust in God to be my light.

Then will I trust, said I, in him alone.
        Nay, ev'n to trust in him, was also his:
        We must confess that nothing is our own.
Then I confess that he my succour is:

But to have nought is ours, not to confess
        That we have nought. I stood amaz'd at this,
        Much troubled, till I heard a friend express,
That all things were more ours by being his.
        What Adam had, and forfeited for all,
        Christ keepeth now, who cannot fail or fall.[1]

1. See Romans 5:12–21 for a summary of what is ours in Adam and what we now have in Christ.

REFLECT

I heard a friend express,
That all things were more ours by being his.

I suspect that all of us who love the Lord and who earnestly long to live more fully for him have experienced something like this. We are overwhelmed by all that God has done for us, and in return, we want to do something for him. He has told us what he wants of us, and so we pledge that we *will* love the Lord our God with all our heart and soul and mind and strength and our neighbor as ourselves . . . if we just try harder, we can do this!

As we soon realize, no, we can't. And just like that, the wind gets taken out of our sails, as it does for the poet when "I was told by one, it could not be." We take stock. OK! If I can't manage that, then at least I will trust wholly in God!

But that isn't ours to accomplish either. We have nothing of our own. As Paul reminds us, we have nothing that we have not first received from God (1 Corinthians 4:7). The very capacity to trust in God is a gift from God.

Well then, how about I simply acknowledge that God alone is my helper? But it is only by God's enabling that we can even do that.

At this point the poet is flabbergasted. Perhaps we are too. Isn't there anything of our own that we can offer to God in gratitude for all that he has given to us?!

No, there isn't! Our Scripture text for this poem, Psalm 116:12–14, hints at this. The psalmist asks what we can return to the Lord for all his goodness to us. The answer is not about what we can do for God, or offer to God, but about continuing to *receive* from God and to call upon God, lifting the cup of salvation and calling on the name of the Lord. And as the friend in this poem would point out, we can only do these things (let alone being able to fulfill our vows to God in Psalm 116:14) because God enables us.

None of this should trouble us in the slightest. Thanks be to God, everything that is good and right about our relationship with God comes to us in and through Christ. Whatever godly wisdom, righteousness, holiness, and redemption is at work in us is first his and then ours because we are "in him" (1 Corinthians 1:30).

Likewise, none of this means that we simply do nothing, as if we stop trying to love God and our neighbor, or as if we stop bothering to thank

God or ask God for anything, or as if we no longer need to acknowledge that God is our help and strength. We keep on doing all those things! What changes is our self-understanding and our posture as we do them. We recognize in humility that left to ourselves we could not be or do any of these things. With deep thankfulness we acknowledge that the inclination and capacity to do them are loving gifts of God's grace.

We do not lose by this, and neither do we become any less ourselves. All of this is to our infinite gain. Genesis 3 tells us of how Adam forfeited the loving relationship with God for which all human beings were created, and left to ourselves we would remain trapped in that spiral of brokenness and alienation from God. In Christ, we and our relationship with God are held secure, and by the Spirit we become more and more who we were created to be in him.

SCRIPTURE: PSALM 116:12–14

DWELL

- Which words, images, or phrases from the poem stand out to you? Ask the Holy Spirit to speak to you through them.
- What thoughts, feelings, or actions are prompted in you as you bring the poem and the Scripture text into conversation with each other? Hold these promptings before God.
- If we're honest, many of us find it hard to fully accept that in our relationship with God, everything is grace and everything is gift, all the way down. In what ways do you find yourself resisting this?
- What difference might it make to how you seek to live more fully for God, to trust God more deeply, and to acknowledge that God is your helper, to realize that it is God himself who is at work in you, fulfilling his good purposes for you, to enable you to do these things (Philippians 2:13)?
- Spend some time prayerfully reflecting on the truth that all things are more ours by first being Christ's. How might your perspective change if you were to think of everything about yourself and your life as belonging first to Christ, and then to you in him?

PRAY

Gracious God, what can I return to you in thankful acknowledgement of your love? I can give nothing to you except what you have already given to me, and already put into my heart to give to you. I know that I have nothing which I have not received, and that without Christ I can do nothing. Left to myself, I cannot even think a good thought, or desire anything good. By your grace, inflame my heart with your love, incite me to perpetual praise and thanksgiving, and kindle in me an everlasting desire to honor you. By your Spirit, who gives me spiritual life and breath, as often as I take a physical breath in, let me receive grace from you, and as often as I breathe out, let me praise you. In Jesus' name, Amen.[2]

GOING FORWARD

Notice—and give thanks for—the work that God has been doing in you through this poem. Be attentive to any next steps God might be inviting you to take.

2. For this prayer I have modernized and adapted the prayers for Monday morning and Tuesday evening in Daniel Featley's *Ancilla Pietatis*. This was a best-selling devotional in Herbert's time.

The Collar

In our previous poem, Herbert threatened to observe every jot and tittle of what God asks of us. Here he is threatening utter rebellion. This is one of the most daring poems Herbert ever wrote, and also one of his best. It is for all of us who have come within a hair's breadth of abandoning our faith and turning to a very different kind of life. It is also for all those of us who have done that, but who have eventually heard and responded to the call of God that Herbert describes here, in yet another of his mic-drop endings.

I struck the board,[1] and cry'd, No more.
I will abroad.
What? Shall I ever sigh and pine?
My lines and life are free;[2] free as the road,
Loose as the wind, as large as store.
Shall I be still in suit?[3]
Have I no harvest but a thorn
To let me blood, and not restore
What I have lost with cordial fruit?
Sure there was wine
Before my sighs did dry it: there was corn
Before my tears did drown it.
Is the year only lost to me?

1. "Board" means the piece of wood that formed the top of a long dining table. This is where we get the phrase "bed [or room] and board" from, meaning a bed/room and meals. Here, as in other poems, it also implies the communion table.

2. "Lines" means poetry. This poem is entirely free form, with no regular rhythm, line length, or rhyming scheme. In his own time, this poem would have been seen as completely chaotic.

3. "Still" means always; "in suit" means petitioning or pleading: "Shall I always be pleading?"

Have I no bays to crown it?[4]
No flowers, no garlands gay? All blasted?
All wasted?
Not so, my heart: but there is fruit,
And thou hast hands.
Recover all thy sigh-blown age
On double pleasures: leave thy cold dispute
Of what is fit, and not. Forsake thy cage,
Thy rope of sands,[5]
Which petty thoughts have made, and made to thee
Good cable, to enforce and draw,
And be thy law,
While thou didst wink and wouldst not see.
Away; take heed:
I will abroad.
Call in thy deaths head there:[6] tie up thy fears.
He that forbears
To suit and serve his need,
Deserves his load.
But as I rav'd and grew more fierce and wild
At every word,
Me thoughts[7] I heard one calling, *Child*:
And I reply'd, *My Lord.*

REFLECT

Me thoughts I heard one calling, Child

Get out of the cage you think you're trapped in. Break free of the pathetic restraints you've put on yourself. What has all this God stuff and church stuff ever done for you, other than tangling you up in repression and shame? You're free. Stop frightening yourself with fairy tales. Live your own life. Do what you want to do. And more fool you if you don't.

Have thoughts like this ever haunted you? The temptation to cease to trust God and to turn aside from his ways to find fulfillment elsewhere is

4. "Bays" signifies the laurel wreath bestowed upon the finest poets in classical times. The idea in these verses is of a wasted year that has seen no success, either in poetry or in life.

5. A rope of sand is proverbial for something useless.

6. A "death's head" is a skull, as a memento mori (a reminder of death)

7. "Me thoughts" means I thought.

as old as Genesis 3, and this is Herbert's most powerful articulation of it. Did you notice the lines "Not so, my heart: but there is fruit, / And thou hast hands"? I think these are the most chilling and sinister words in all of Herbert's poetry. They are meant to take us straight to the first sin. It is as if the voice of the serpent has taken over, until the voice of God breaks through at the very end.

And just like the serpent's words to Eve in Genesis 3, the thoughts of rebellion here are carefully curated to Herbert's situation. As we have seen in other poems, Herbert went through times when he was deeply frustrated that his life seemed to be going nowhere, and when he was struggling to keep hold of faith and trust through major disappointments. We have also seen his distress at times when he felt that God was either absent or utterly indifferent. All of that is reflected in the temptations in this poem.

These temptations are also based on what are at best only half-truths. "There has been nothing but pain and loss to show for all my efforts!" is Herbert's outraged complaint. Yet there *has* been good fruit; it was his own attitude that spoiled it. Herbert doesn't want to dwell on that, though. What he wants to hear is how God's ways are holding him back from all the pleasures and all the gains that would otherwise be his if he could just break free and stop worrying about what is right and wrong in God's sight. Half-truths make us captive to huge lies.

The poem itself is all over the place. There is no regular rhyming scheme, rhythm, or line length. For seventeenth-century readers this would have indicated, as much as the words themselves, that the poet was "raving." The breakdown in poetic form depicts a poetic persona in meltdown.

And then the voice of God calls him back. Notice what God says. It's not a command. It's not a word of warning or condemnation. It's an expression of loving relationship: "Child." Herbert's response is a relational one too: "My Lord." This is not just about recognizing God as his master. It is about returning to the one whom he knows to be his loving Lord and Savior.

Although we have to wait until the final lines to hear it directly, the redemptive love of the Lord has been present throughout the poem. The "board" that Herbert defiantly strikes at the start is the Lord's table—the communion table—and the fruit that he has spoiled turns out to be the elements of the Lord's Supper. When Herbert complains that his only harvest is a thorn that draws blood from him, rather than the crown of praise he had hoped for, we find echoes of the suffering love of Christ for us in his crown of thorns.

The title itself is loaded with double meanings. The "collar" might signify the yoke worn by oxen or draft horses to pull a load. If it does, it is at once the restraint that Herbert wants to throw off, and it reminds us of Jesus' saying that his yoke is easy and his burden is light (Matthew 11:30). (One thing it does *not* mean, however, is the white collar that clergy sometimes wear. Clerical collars like that don't appear until two centuries after Herbert's death!) With what we know of seventeenth-century pronunciation, "collar" would also have sounded very like "choler" (anger), which is the state the poet is in for most of the poem, and also "caller," which points us to the loving and gentle call of God at the end.

Even in the very midst of our worst spiritual kicking and screaming we are gently held and deeply loved. In Christ, God has taken upon himself all our hurt, all our rebellion, everything that we have done and could ever do to try to break away from God, so that once again we might know ourselves as who we most truly are: beloved children of God.

SCRIPTURE: LUKE 15:11–32

DWELL

- Which words, images, or phrases from the poem stand out to you? Ask the Holy Spirit to speak to you through them.
- What thoughts, feelings, or actions are prompted in you as you bring the poem and the Scripture text into conversation with each other? Hold these promptings before God.
- The temptations to turn away from God in this poem are connected to the circumstances in Herbert's life and discipleship that he finds most difficult and frustrating. Ask the Holy Spirit to help you to acknowledge what those circumstances are in your own life, and to keep you alert to the equivalent temptations.
- Have you ever been assailed by the kinds of thoughts that Herbert articulates in the second half of this poem: that faith and discipleship are lies and nonsense to scare you away from being and doing whatever you want? If so, what held you back from forsaking the Lord's ways? Or, if you took that path, what brought you back?
- Even in our fiercest rebellion God does not break relationship with us. Look back on the rebellious times in your life and reflect on how God

called to you in the midst of them. Give thanks for God's tenaciously faithful love toward you.

PRAY

O to grace how great a debtor
daily I'm constrained to be!
Let thy goodness, like a fetter,
bind my wandering heart to thee.
Prone to wander, Lord, I feel it,
prone to leave the God I love;
here's my heart, O take and seal it,
seal it for thy courts above.[8]

GOING FORWARD

Notice—and give thanks for—the work that God has been doing in you through this poem. Be attentive to any next steps God might be inviting you to take.

8. This prayer is a stanza of Robert Robinson's hymn "Come, Thou Fount of Every Blessing": https://hymnary.org/text/come_thou_fount_of_every_blessing.

Assurance

After our previous poem of rebellion, which ends with the loving call of God and Herbert's response, here we have a poem of deep reassurance. Questions related to our assurance of salvation were a major issue in Herbert's time. Theologians and pastors addressed them in academic treatises and in what we'd now call "Christian living" books. Herbert gives both a theological and a pastoral response in this poem, depicting himself as a bullied child who runs to his Father for all the comfort and protection he needs.

O spiteful bitter thought!
Bitterly spiteful thought! Couldst thou invent
So high a torture? Is such poison bought?[1]
Doubtless, but in the way of punishment,
When wit contrives to meet with thee,
No such rank poison can there be.[2]

Thou said'st but even now,
That all was not so fair as I conceiv'd
Betwixt my God and me; that I allow
And coin large hopes, but that I was deceiv'd:[3]
Either the league was broke, or near it;[4]
And that I had great cause to fear it.

1. "Is such poison bought?" seems to be the poet asking whether he has done something to cause this. He acknowledges that he has ("doubtless"), which is why this comes as a punishment, rather than the spiteful thought simply inventing its poisonous accusation.

2. When reason (wit) joins up with the spiteful thought (to further it) there cannot be a fouler poison.

3. The suggestion is that Herbert is minting counterfeit coins/hopes for himself.

4. The "league" is the covenant between God and himself.

And what to this? what more
Could poison, if it had a tongue, express?[5]
What is thy aim? Wouldst thou unlock the door
To cold despairs, and gnawing pensiveness?
Wouldst thou raise devils? I see, I know,
I writ thy purpose long ago.[6]

But I will to my Father,
Who heard thee say it. O most gracious Lord,
If all the hope and comfort that I gather,
Were from my self, I had not half a word,
Not half a letter to oppose
What is objected by my foes.

But thou art my desert:[7]
And in this league, which now my foes invade,
Thou art not only to perform thy part,
But also mine;[8] as when the league was made
Thou didst at once thy self indite,[9]
And hold my hand, while I did write.

Wherefore if thou canst fail,
Then can thy truth and I: but while rocks stand,
And rivers stir, thou canst not shrink or quail:
Yea, when both rocks and all things shall disband,
Then shalt thou be my rock and tower,
And make their ruin praise thy power.

5. What could be worse than this? If poison had a tongue, what more could it say than this?

6. Herbert knows all about this. He has written poems about what happens when you give in to this way of thinking.

7. "Desert" means merit or deserving. God himself is the only reason that Herbert deserves anything good from the covenant.

8. God not only plays his part in the covenant, but he also takes our part upon himself in Christ, especially on the cross.

9. "Indite" has two senses here. On the cross Christ both inscribes himself into the covenant, paying our debt, and he is indicted (condemned). As Herbert goes on to say, God even helps us to "sign on" to the new covenant in Christ, so to speak—he enables us to come to faith, which is how we enter into it.

Now foolish thought go on,
Spin out thy thread, and make thereof a coat
To hide thy shame: for thou hast cast a bone
Which bounds on thee, and will not down thy throat:[10]
What for itself love once began,
Now love and truth will end in man.[11]

REFLECT

But I will to my Father

Have you ever been bullied? Has someone you love been the victim of bullying? In this poem, the bully is a deeply hurtful personified thought that is trying to make Herbert doubt his salvation. This thought tells him that he's deluded if he thinks that all is well between him and God. In fact, God has more or less given up on him.

Herbert sees this poisonous thought for what it is: the equivalent of the serpent in Genesis 3 trying to persuade him that he is deceived about God's love and care for him. In particular, this thought is trying to make Herbert look to himself as the basis of his assurance. But Herbert knows what many of us also know all too well: that train of thought will lead us into an endless cycle of destructive spiritual introspection. We will always be trying to find ways to prove to ourselves that we really are all right with God, but the evidence of our messed-up selves will only lead us to further doubts. As Herbert says, if the source of his assurance were himself and his life, then the nasty thought would be right: his relationship with God would be on very thin ice.

But Herbert knows what to do. His response is exactly right, theologically, scripturally, spiritually, existentially. He runs to his Father for all the assurance he needs: "I will go to my Father! He heard what you said!"

As many theologians and pastors in Herbert's time pointed out, our primary source of assurance lies not in ourselves but in the unshakable promises of God. God's covenant with us can no more fail than God can cease to be God. Even if the earth gives way and the mountains fall into the sea, the Lord's unfailing covenant love will remain, and he will be our strength and fortress (e.g., Psalm 46; Isaiah 54:10).

10. The image is of the thought attempting to get Herbert to choke on a bone but getting it stuck in its own throat.

11. "End" means reach its purpose. What God began out of love will culminate in demonstrating his love and truth for and in us, e.g., Philippians 1:6.

The bullying thought has been defeated the moment Herbert turns to his Father. It is the Holy Spirit himself who enables us to cry "Abba! Father!" and this in itself is a sign of God's love for us. When we do this, the Spirit is bearing witness with us that we are God's beloved children (Romans 8:14–17).

What's more, we know that we can wholly trust God's love for us because he has taken the whole burden of our side of the covenant upon himself in Christ, and he even helps us to respond. Left to ourselves we couldn't "sign on" to the covenant, but God guides our hand, so to speak. In a beautifully tender image, Herbert depicts God as a father teaching him how to write.

With all of this true assurance, the deceitful thought is exposed as foolish and harmless. It can go on spinning its lies into a coat to hide its shame, like the fig leaves Adam and Eve used to cover theirs. Herbert knows that he and we can trust in the unassailable love and faithfulness of God. He is safe in his Father's arms, and so are we.

SCRIPTURE: PSALM 46

DWELL

- Which words, images, or phrases from the poem stand out to you? Ask the Holy Spirit to speak to you through them.
- What thoughts, feelings, or actions are prompted in you as you bring the poem and the Scripture text into conversation with each other? Hold these promptings before God.
- Some of us struggle with the scriptural language of God as Father. Herbert's depiction here is deeply loving and tender. God is the one to whom he can run for protection from bullies, with all his hurts and fears, and the one who holds his hand to teach him to write. Take to God what this evokes in you of love, gratitude, hurt, or longing, and ask God to show you how he is all that you need him to be.
- Have you had times of doubting whether you truly belong to God? Do you instinctively look within yourself to try to find enough evidence to resolve those doubts? Ask the Holy Spirit to help you to look not to yourself, but to Christ who has taken your part and reconciled you to the Father.

- When we are wrapped up in our anxieties, we can sometimes forget the magnitude of the promises and faithfulness of God. Take some time to dwell with the idea that God's *hesed* (his covenant love and faithfulness) is more unshakable than the very foundations of the earth. Let this help to shape your perspective on your concerns.

PRAY

Loving God,
what fellowship, what joy
what blessedness, what peace it is
to lean on your everlasting arms.
There is nothing to dread, nothing to fear.
Nothing can do me ultimate harm.
I trust myself wholly to you,
safe and secure because you are near,
and I am held in your everlasting arms.[12]

GOING FORWARD

Notice—and give thanks for—the work that God has been doing in you through this poem. Be attentive to any next steps God might be inviting you to take.

12. For this prayer I have drawn on the words of E. A. Hoffman's hymn "Leaning on the Everlasting Arms": https://hymnary.org/text/what_a_fellowship_what_a_joy_divine.

The Call

How can a poem that seems so simple be so beautiful and so profound? Every word except one has just a single syllable, but what words they are! They are some of the richest that Scripture has given us, starting with Jesus' words about himself in John 14:6. Herbert then builds these words up into an intimate portrait of Christ's love for us as our Creator and Redeemer.

Come, my Way, my Truth, my Life:[1]
Such a Way as gives us breath;
Such a Truth as ends all strife;
Such a Life as killeth death.

Come, my Light,[2] my Feast, my Strength:
Such a Light as shows a feast;
Such a Feast as mends in length;[3]
Such a Strength as makes his guest.

Come, my Joy, my Love, my Heart:
Such a Joy as none can move;[4]
Such a Love as none can part;[5]
Such a Heart as joys in love.[6]

1. John 14:6.

2. John 1:4; 8:12.

3. "Mends in length" means gets better as it goes on. The feast here points us to the Lord's Supper now and to the eschatological marriage feast of the Lamb that is to come.

4. "None can move" means that no one can change.

5. Romans 8:31–39: nothing can separate us from the love of God in Christ.

6. "Joys in love" means rejoices in love.

REFLECT

Come, my Joy, my Love, my Heart

Go back to the whole of that last stanza for a moment, with what it has to say about who Christ is to you and who you are to Christ. He is your joy, your love, your heart, and his heart rejoices so much in you that nothing can separate you from his love. Is there anything more beautiful than this?

I love this poem so much! It is one of the most sheerly joyful poems Herbert ever wrote. It is both a prayer to Christ and a love poem, and it is filled with such wondrous words about Christ that you could spend any amount of time dwelling on each one. But there is also an intricate beauty in how Herbert weaves them together until we end up with that last stanza, in which Christ's heart and ours are ecstatically rejoicing together in love.

The one who is our Way has given us our breath for the journey. He is the one who breathed into us the breath of life (Genesis 2:7) and breathed upon us the breath of new life (John 20:22). The Way is also the Truth, and to fully know and follow that Truth will be the end of all strife. It will be the fullness of shalom, which is the flourishing that will come when we and all things are in right relationship with God and one another. That will be a reality only in the fullness of eternal life, made possible because Christ who is Life has destroyed death. The only word with more than one syllable is here, to emphasize the magnitude of what Christ has done: he is the Life that "killeth death."

Jesus is the Light of the world (John 8:12). That light shows us a feast, and not just any feast. It is the Feast that embodies our union and communion with Christ himself: the Lord's Supper, which is a foretaste of the marriage feast of the Lamb. It is a feast now and into eternity that gets better and better as it goes along. In the meanwhile, as food nourishes and strengthens our bodies, so feasting on Christ nourishes and strengthens our faith. But Christ who is our Strength doesn't just strengthen us. He is the one who made us, and by his life, death, and resurrection, has made us fit to be his beloved guests to all eternity.

Finally, Christ is "my Joy, my Love, my Heart." The glorious truth of this final stanza is that nothing can change Christ's joy in us (e.g., Hebrews 12:2) and his love for us. In our union with Christ, this also means that nothing can take this foundational joy from us (e.g., John 16:22) or separate us from his love (Romans 8:35–39). And while the two stanzas before this one led us from one word to the next, notice that in the final line Herbert brings all three of these words together in a beautiful culmination to the whole poem: such a *heart* as *joys* in *love.*

SCRIPTURE: JOHN 1:1–9; 6:53–58; 8:12; 14:6

Many verses from John's Gospel are echoed in this poem. Here are some of them. You might like to spend time with each one, or just focus on a couple.

DWELL

- Which words, images, or phrases from the poem stand out to you? Ask the Holy Spirit to speak to you through them.
- What thoughts, feelings, or actions are prompted in you as you bring the poem and the Scripture text/s into conversation with each other? Hold those promptings before God.
- Choose a word or phrase that makes you say to yourself, "I wouldn't have thought of that!" Dwell with it for a while to see what it might teach you about Christ and your relationship with him.
- Christ loves you and rejoices in you with all his heart. Take time to let that sink in. Then go to Christ with your response—and ask him what it might look like for your heart to love and rejoice in him more and more fully too.
- Choose some words of your own to describe who Christ is for you. Don't worry about trying to weave them together as intricately as Herbert does! Simply write a sentence on each of them, describing what those words mean for your relationship with Christ.

PRAY

Dearest Lord Jesus, you are the way to all who go to you, the truth to all who know you, the life to all who believe in you. Fill me with joy in you, that I may embrace you with love and live continually in your presence until your second coming. Come to me, Lord Jesus, come quickly. Amen.[7]

7. For this prayer I have adapted Daniel Featley's prayer for Christmas Day in his *Ancilla Pietatis.*

GOING FORWARD

Notice—and give thanks for—the work that God has been doing in you through this poem. Be attentive to any next steps God might be inviting you to take.

Clasping of Hands

This is a playful and witty poem about something profoundly beautiful: "my beloved is mine and I am his" (Song of Songs 2:16 KJV). Don't be put off by how confusing the poem seems, with all those dizzying "mines" and "thines" until you aren't sure whom Herbert is referring to anymore. That's the point, as you'll see in the final line!

Lord, thou art mine, and I am thine,[1]
If mine I am: and thine much more,
Than I or ought, or can be mine.
Yet to be thine, doth me restore;
So that again I now am mine,
And with advantage mine the more,
Since this being mine, brings with it thine,
And thou with me dost thee restore.
    If I without thee would be mine,
    I neither should be mine nor thine.

1. Because this is a rather convoluted poem, here is a paraphrase that might help you to follow it. This doesn't remotely capture all the teasing wit and ambiguous complexity of Herbert's own words, though, so just use it as a guide, and then go right back to the fun of Herbert's intricate wordplay!

> Lord, you are mine and I am yours, if I am to be mine; and I am yours far more than I either ought to be or can be my own. Yet to be yours restores me, so that I am now mine again, and even more mine, since this way of being mine brings you along with it. And you restoring me restores you too [Herbert is drawing on the idea that we are members of Christ's body]. If I would be mine apart from you, then I would be neither mine nor yours.
>
> Lord, I am yours and you are mine. You are so much mine that I may presume you to be more mine than your own. For you suffered to restore not yourself but me, and in order to be mine—even more mine, since in your death you gave up your very self, but in being mine you restored me. O be mine always! Always make me yours! Or rather make it so there is no yours and mine.

Lord, I am thine, and thou art mine:
So mine thou art, that something more
I may presume thee mine, than thine.
For thou didst suffer to restore
Not thee, but me, and to be mine,
And with advantage mine the more,
Since thou in death wast none of thine,
Yet then as mine didst me restore.
        O be mine still! Still make me thine!
        Or rather make no Thine and Mine!

REFLECT

O be mine still! Still make me thine!
Or rather make no Thine and Mine!

Think about the title for a moment. When we clasp someone by the hand—when we join hands and twine fingers with someone—our hands are so bound together that it is hard to tell whose is whose! That could be a visual representation of the intricately tangled wordplay of "mine/thine" in this poem.

There is profound intimacy in holding hands in this way. It is something we do only with someone we deeply love and trust. Christ taking him by the hand is one of Herbert's favorite images for Christ's intimate love. We saw it in "Easter" and "The Dawning" and we will see it again, most beautifully of all, in the final poem, "Love (III)."

By calling this poem "Clasping of Hands" I wonder if Herbert intended to evoke the idea of the "handfast"—the custom of an engaged couple clasping hands to indicate their betrothal. The verse from the Song of Songs (2:16) which prompts the poem might suggest that too. From the early days of the church, the physical intimacy of this scriptural love poem was interpreted as symbolizing the union of Christ the Bridegroom with the church as his bride, and of Christ and the individual Christian.

Theologians speak of this loving union between Christ and us, in which he is ours and we are his, as the "wondrous exchange," and they often draw on marriage imagery to describe it. Christ takes upon himself the sin and death that we bring to the relationship, and gives us what is his: love, joy, peace, and reconciliation with God.

Everything about the intricate construction of this poem is Herbert playfully seeking to encapsulate something of the wonder and mystery of our union with Christ. So, for example, look at the last word of each line across both stanzas. And then, notice the repeated line: "And with advantage mine the more." This is the heart of it. As we belong to Christ, we become more fully our true selves than we could possibly be apart from him.

This recalls the first question and answer of the Heidelberg Catechism once again. We encountered it earlier when we reflected on "The Dialogue." It declares that our only comfort in life and in death is that "I am not my own but belong . . . to my faithful savior Jesus Christ." Our prayer for this poem, from the Methodist tradition, begins similarly: "I am not my own but thine." It ends by echoing the same words from the Song of Songs that inspired Herbert to write this poem. All of these voices are calling us to remember that who we most truly are is found in belonging to Christ, and in the beautiful reciprocity of the love by which he is ours and we are his.

SCRIPTURE: GALATIANS 2:20

DWELL

- Which words, images, or phrases from the poem stand out to you? Ask the Holy Spirit to speak to you through them.
- What thoughts, feelings, or actions are prompted in you as you bring the poem and the Scripture text into conversation with each other? Hold these promptings before God.
- Imagine Christ clasping your hand, and you clasping his. What thoughts and feelings arise within you?
- As this poem reminds us, to be united to Christ makes us more truly ourselves, and we cannot be our true selves apart from him. Ponder with Christ what it might mean for you to discover more and more of who you truly are in him.
- What difference might it make to your daily life and your relationships with others to see your identity primarily as someone who belongs to Christ, and who loves him and is loved by him?

PRAY

In addition to the prayer below, you might like to listen to the gloriously playful and intimate duet "Mein Freund ist mein," from Bach's Cantata

BWV 140 (*Wachet auf*). This is a musical setting of the same verse that inspired Herbert's poem (Song of Songs 2:16) and it captures something of the spirit of Herbert's poem too!

I am no longer mine own but thine.
Put me to what thou wilt, rank me with whom thou wilt;
put me to doing, put me to suffering;
let me be employed by thee, or laid aside for thee,
exalted for thee, or brought low for thee;
let me be full, let me be empty,
let me have all things, let me have nothing:
I freely and wholeheartedly yield all things
to thy pleasure and disposal.
And now, O glorious and blessed God,
Father, Son, and Holy Spirit,
thou are mine and I am thine. So be it.
And the covenant which I have made on earth,
let it be ratified in heaven.
Amen.[2]

GOING FORWARD

Notice—and give thanks for—the work that God has been doing in you through this poem. Be attentive to any next steps God might be inviting you to take.

2. This prayer is central to the annual covenant renewal service in Methodist churches, and many other denominations have adopted it as well. Contemporary versions replace "thine" with "yours" (and make other changes to the wording too), but I have used John Wesley's original prayer, published in 1780, to make a clearer connection with Herbert's poem.

The Flower

This is one of Herbert's most famous and beloved poems, bringing together many themes in his poetry as a whole. In it he depicts the various seasons in our relationship with God through the analogy of the life cycle of a perennial flower, and anticipates the new creation, where no flower can wither and we will abide in the love of God forever.

How fresh, O Lord, how sweet and clean
Are thy returns! even as the flowers in spring;
To which, besides their own demean,[1]
The late-past frosts tributes of pleasure bring.
Grief melts away
Like snow in May,
As if there were no such cold thing.

Who would have thought my shrivel'd heart
Could have recover'd greenness? It was gone
Quite underground; as flowers depart
To see their mother-root, when they have blown,
Where they together
All the hard weather,
Dead to the world, keep house unknown.

These are thy wonders, Lord of power,
Killing and quickening,[2] bringing down to hell
And up to heaven in an hour;

1. "Demean" signifies demeanor/appearance. The idea in these two lines is that in addition to their lovely appearance, the flowers signify the welcome end of frosts and winter.

2. "Quickening" means bringing to life.

Making a chiming of a passing-bell.[3]
We say amiss
This or that is:
Thy word is all, if we could spell.[4]

O that I once past changing were,
Fast in thy Paradise,[5] where no flower can wither!
Many a spring I shoot up fair,
Offering at heaven, growing and groaning thither;
Nor doth my flower
Want a spring shower,[6]
My sins and I joining together.

But while I grow in a straight line,
Still upwards bent, as if heaven were mine own,
Thy anger comes, and I decline:
What frost to that? what pole is not the zone
Where all things burn,[7]
When thou dost turn,
And the least frown of thine is shown?

And now in age I bud again,
After so many deaths I live and write;
I once more smell the dew and rain,
And relish versing. Oh, my only light,
It cannot be
That I am he
On whom thy tempests fell all night.

These are thy wonders, Lord of love,
To make us see we are but flowers that glide;[8]
Which when we once can find and prove,

3. A "passing bell" is the bell rung at a death or for a funeral, so the idea here is: making the grim tolling of a death bell into a pleasant chiming.

4. God's word is everything, if we could interpret it properly.

5. "Fast" means secure.

6. To "want" here means to lack. The idea is that his flower doesn't lack a spring shower because of his tears for his sins.

7. There is nothing in the world that feels so cold as when God is angry with us. The Arctic and Antarctic Poles feel like the equator in comparison to that.

8. "Glide" means fade away.

Thou hast a garden for us where to bide;[9]
Who would be more,
Swelling through store,[10]
Forfeit their Paradise by their pride.

REFLECT

Who would have thought my shrivel'd heart
Could have recover'd greenness?

Where do you see yourself within this poem? Which images and ideas resonate most with your experiences of life and faith?

Perhaps you connect with Herbert's descriptions of times of refreshing, like the first blooming of spring flowers, when you are relishing a feeling of new spiritual life in the loving presence of God after a season of dullness.

Many of us have also experienced times when we have had to pull back and hunker down, like a flower that returns to its roots for the winter. Those are hard seasons, and yet there can be a sense of sheltering and comfort in the midst of them, and a gathering of strength to be able to reemerge later.

Thinking back to "The Temper (I)," you might relate to Herbert's experience here of being stretched by the extremes in his relationship with God, who can bring "down to hell / And up to heaven in an hour." You might also connect with his account of being someone "on whom thy tempests fell all night."

This is one of Herbert's later poems. When he writes about similar experiences earlier in his life, there is often a great deal of anguish and struggle. Here, he still feels strongly. There is his trademark deep emotional honesty, which give us permission to express all that we are feeling to God as well. But there is also a more mature wisdom. While we live through the "changes and chances of this mortal life" (1662 BCP communion service), and while we have to deal with the implications of sin in ourselves and in others, there will be fluctuating seasons in our relationship with God. Although the pain still runs deep, Herbert seems more ready to accept that bitter seasons of God's apparent absence will remain as much a part of the way that God deals with him as the longed-for returns to an awareness

9. When we realize and accept that we fade like the flowers, God has a (heavenly) garden for us where we will abide/remain forever.

10. Being puffed up with what they have acquired.

of God's loving presence. As this poem suggests, God brings little deaths and resurrections into our lives, and is mysteriously at work for us in and through both.

Herbert suggests that this is one way in which the Lord of love cultivates a proper perspective in us, and a true hope. Our earthly lives are as transient as the flowers of the field (Psalm 103:15–16; Isaiah 40:6–8), yet at the same time, we are also the beloved of God, who has prepared an eternal inheritance for us that will never perish or fade (1 Peter 1:4). By God's grace, the various seasons in our lives and our faith are preparing us for an eternity of experiencing the fullness of God's unchanging love.

SCRIPTURE: PSALM 103

DWELL

- Which words, images, or phrases from the poem stand out to you? Ask the Holy Spirit to speak to you through them.
- What thoughts, feelings, or actions are prompted in you as you bring the poem and the Scripture text into conversation with each other? Hold these promptings before God.
- Reflect on the seasons in your life when your heart has felt dry and shriveled, or when you have had to withdraw and "go underground," or when it has felt like the Lord has been buffeting you with storms. What difference does it make to situate those experiences within the cycle of the "seasons" in your relationship with God?
- For Herbert one of the signs of renewed life is when he is able to relish writing poetry again. What are the signs of "recovered greenness" in your life, and in your relationship with God?
- This is a poem that helps us to realize both that our earthly lives are as fleeting as a flower's and also that we are destined to bloom eternally, so to speak. How does this help you to find perspective on the specifics of your life and your walk with God?

PRAY

> Merciful Lord, restore to me the joy of your salvation! Do not cast me out from your presence, and do not take your Holy Spirit from me. Create a clean heart within me and renew a steadfast and willing spirit within me to sustain me, that I might rejoice in you and lead others in your ways. In Jesus' name. Amen.[11]

GOING FORWARD

Notice—and give thanks for—the work that God has been doing in you through this poem. Be attentive to any next steps God might be inviting you to take.

11. I wrote this prayer based on verses from Psalm 51.

A True Hymn

An underlying theme in Herbert's poetry is the relationship between artistry and sincerity. Herbert was a superbly inventive poet who wanted to offer his very best to God, but he also knew that what God values most is not poetic skill but his heart, and not cleverness but love. Here is a poem about all of that, which is also deeply encouraging for those of us who aren't brilliant poets!

My joy, my life, my crown!
My heart was meaning all the day,
Somewhat it fain would say:[1]
And still it runneth mutt'ring up and down
With only this, *My joy, my life, my crown.*

Yet slight not these few words:[2]
If truly said, they may take part
Among the best in art.
The fineness which a hymn or psalm affords,
Is when the soul unto the lines accords.

He who craves all the mind,
And all the soul, and strength, and time,
If the words only rhyme,
Justly complains, that somewhat is behind
To make his verse, or write a hymn in kind.[3]

1. There has been something on his heart all day that it has been longing to say.

2. "Slight not" means do not despise.

3. God desires our whole selves (Herbert is riffing on Jesus' summary of the first and greatest commandment to love the Lord our God with all our heart and soul and mind and strength), so he will justly complain that if the verse or hymn we write has only rhyming words, then it is missing the most important part of making it a true hymn.

Whereas if th'heart be moved,
Although the verse be somewhat scant,
God doth supply the want.[4]
As when th'heart says (sighing to be approved)
O, could I love! and stops: God writeth, *Loved.*

REFLECT

God doth supply the want.

We all know the frustration of not being able find the word we need. It's on the tip of my tongue, we sometimes say. And we know the anxiety of desperately wanting to be able to say the right thing to someone, and the disappointment that follows if the words don't come out the way we intended.

Here, Herbert's heart has something important to say to God, but all it can come up with is "My joy, my life, my crown!" As he points out, though, it doesn't matter if your words don't seem to be adequate. The most important thing is that your words and your soul align, and that your heart is in them. If the words merely rhyme but aren't an expression of your whole self, then the most important part is missing. There's a sly poetic joke in the third stanza. Jesus' summary of the greatest commandment in Mark 12:30 is that we are to love the Lord our God with all our *heart*, soul, mind, and strength, but heart doesn't rhyme, and time does. . . . The very structure of the poem makes the point of the stanza: mere rhyme is unimportant to God without our heart.

On the other hand, if your words express your wholehearted desire to love and live for God, then it doesn't matter how simple they are, or how feeble your poem is! You have just written the finest hymn in the world as far as God is concerned, and he will make up whatever is lacking.

You might have noticed some huge ironies here! Herbert starts out by asking us not to mock what he fears might be the rather poor material his heart has provided for his poem. He goes on to write a very clever and skillful poem (in terms of poetic technique, this is virtuoso stuff) about how God doesn't want or need clever and skillful poems. And then, this is a poem about writing poems. The actual "true hymn" of the title and of his heart—"My joy, my life, my crown"—all but disappears.

4. If our hearts are moved then even if our poetry isn't much good, God will supply what is lacking (in Herbert's time, "want" meant lack as well as desire).

I wonder if Herbert nails the heart of it in his aside in the second to last line, where he speaks of how the heart sighs to be approved. We crave approval. We long to be loved. So much of what we say and do is driven by the desire for God and others to please notice me, please tell me I mean something to you, please love me . . .

Everything from the false humility of the start (those are good, rich, scriptural words! There is no need to apologize for them!) to the humblebrag of the entire poem, and its tussle between poetic artistry and a sincere heart, boils down to a deep longing for God's approval and love. It's as if this whole poem is summed up in that hesitant half sentence: "O, I wish I could love . . ." to which God instantly replies, "You are loved."

We don't need to be anxious about either earning or losing God's approval and love. God's love has already had the first word. The only way that we could make even the first move toward loving God is because God loved us first (1 John 4:19). And as Herbert beautifully demonstrates here, God's love has the last word too.

SCRIPTURE: PSALM 63:3–4

DWELL

- Which words, images, or phrases from the poem stand out to you? Ask the Holy Spirit to speak to you through them.
- What thoughts, feelings, or actions are prompted in you as you bring the poem and the Scripture text into conversation with each other? Hold these promptings before God.
- There's a lot of pressure on all of us to present a perfect veneer to the world. We're afraid that any signs of inadequacy might destroy our credibility. What difference might it make if you were to allow simplicity, sincerity, and "this isn't brilliant, but it's the best I can come up with right now" to be enough?
- Reflect with God on how much of what you say and do is driven by your desire for approval. Ask God to help you to let go of whatever fears are driving that desire, and to accept that you are loved.
- Consider writing your own heartfelt "true hymn." It doesn't have to be a poem. Write whatever words express your love to God in whatever form you like! As Herbert reminds us here, don't worry if you don't

think it is very good! If it expresses your heart, it will bring delight to God.

PRAY

Beautiful Savior, King of creation,
Son of God and Son of Man,
Truly I'd love thee, truly I'd serve thee,
Light of my soul, my joy, my crown.

Beautiful Savior, Lord of the Nations,
Son of God and Son of Man,
Glory and honor, praise, adoration,
Now and forevermore be thine.[5]

GOING FORWARD

Notice—and give thanks for—the work that God has been doing in you through this poem. Be attentive to any next steps God might be inviting you to take.

5. Originally appearing anonymously in the late seventeenth century, these are the first and last stanzas of a hymn known in various translations as "Beautiful Savior" or "Fairest Lord Jesus": https://hymnary.org/text/beautiful_savior_king_of_creation.

Bitter-Sweet

In these eight short lines Herbert sums up so many of the paradoxes in our relationship with God. In some ways it's a companion piece to "Justice (I)," which we reflected on earlier. Here, though, Herbert doesn't give any explanations. He simply describes what it is like to live in the tension of apparent opposites.

Ah, my dear angry Lord,
Since thou dost love, yet strike;
Cast down, yet help afford;
Sure I will do the like.[1]

I will complain, yet praise;
I will bewail, approve;[2]
And all my sour-sweet days
I will lament, and love.

REFLECT

And all my sour-sweet days
I will lament, and love.

Does the opening of this poem make you feel uncomfortable? Many of us struggle with the idea of God's anger. At times, Herbert did too. Another of his poems, "Discipline," opens with the words, "Throw away thy rod, Lord /

1. "Sure I will do the like" means I will surely do similarly.

2. To "bewail" is to express bitter disappointment; "approve" means express approval of.

Throw away thy wrath." Even so, he is being honest both to the language of Scripture and to the reality of our experience. This is part of the complexity that goes along with being beloved and sinful creatures in a relationship with our loving and holy God. As our reflections on "Justice (I)" reminded us, our experience of human relationships will also color how we respond to language like this about our relationship with God.

This poem might make us feel uncomfortable in another way too. From the title onwards, Herbert is inviting us to sit with all sorts of tensions. He simply states them, with no attempt to resolve them.

Herbert is being honest to reality in this as well, because we are going to be sitting in these kinds of tensions for the rest of our earthly lives. The biblical scholars speak of how we are living in the "in-between time": the tension between the "already" of the victory Christ has won and the "not yet" of his return in glory, when sin and death will finally be no more. We see this on a grand scale in the world around us. Here, Herbert is expressing that reality on the very intimate scale of our own little lives, and our relationship with God.

There is something else for us to notice here which is crucial to the poem. While there are indeed major poles of tension, so to speak, the force field that holds them together is love: first God's love toward Herbert, and then Herbert's toward God.

So, it is his "dear Lord" who is angry, and it is *because* Herbert knows he is loved that he asks for the Lord's correction. This echoes our Scripture text for this poem (Proverbs 3:11–12, which is quoted in Hebrews 12:5–6 and Revelation 3:19). It is those whom God loves that he rebukes and chastens. The one who casts us down will also raise us up. In turn, Herbert's response to God will be just as full of apparent opposites, but love literally has the last word. For all the tensions that Herbert holds in this poem, everything comes from love and leads to love.

SCRIPTURE: PROVERBS 3:11–12

DWELL

- Which words, images, or phrases from the poem stand out to you? Ask the Holy Spirit to speak to you through them.

- What thoughts, feelings, or actions are prompted in you as you bring the poem and the Scripture text into conversation with each other? Hold these promptings before God.
- Simply acknowledging and sitting in tension can be very hard. What have you learned when you have done this? What are some of the ways that you have tried to avoid it?
- Do Herbert's pairs of apparent opposites reflect your experience of life with God? What others might you include?
- It is extremely important to recognize that all the tensions we feel in our relationship with God are held together in love. Take some time to dwell with that thought, and the difference it makes to how you experience your life with God.

PRAY

Lord my God, when my heart is heavy I will complain to you.
When I am cast down I wonder if you have forgotten me,
or whether, in your anger, you have forgotten your mercy.
But then I remember the wonders you have done,
and I praise you for your mighty saving deeds.
Lead me, I pray, in the paths of your redeeming love.
Amen.[3]

GOING FORWARD

Notice—and give thanks for—the work that God has been doing in you through this poem. Be attentive to any next steps God might be inviting you to take.

3. I wrote this prayer based on verses from Psalm 77.

The Glance

This poem might particularly resonate with those of us who have been Christians for a while and have experienced many seasons in our Christian life. I suspect that all of us will connect with one of the most beautiful and moving lines in all of Herbert's poetry, as he anticipates the overwhelming wonder and joy of beholding Christ face-to-face in glory, when he will "look us out of pain."

When first thy sweet and gracious eye
Vouchsaf'd[1] ev'n in the midst of youth and night
To look upon me, who before did lie
Weltring in sin;[2]
I felt a sugar'd strange delight,
Passing all cordials made by any art,[3]
Bedew, embalm, and overrun my heart,[4]
And take it in.[5]

1. To "vouchsafe" is to graciously condescend.

2. "Weltring" (weltering) means wallowing.

3. Cordials were sweetened medicinal drinks.

4. "Bedew" means sprinkle; to "embalm" is to anoint with oil; "overrun" means overflow.

5. When Herbert says that the delight of the Lord's glance "took in" his heart, it means captivated, but there's a lurking sense of being deceived. This poem is an older, wiser echo of an earlier poem, "Affliction (I)," which even begins similarly ("When first thou didst entice to thee my heart"), and in which Herbert accused God of deceiving him, because everything was rosy at the start, and he expected things would always be like that . . . but that was not how it turned out.

Since that time many a bitter storm
My soul hath felt, ev'n able to destroy,
Had the malicious and ill-meaning harm
His swing and sway:[6]
But still thy sweet original joy,
Sprung from thine eye, did work within my soul,
And surging griefs, when they grew bold, control,
And got the day.

If thy first glance so powerful be,
A mirth but open'd and seal'd up again;[7]
What wonders shall we feel, when we shall see
Thy full-ey'd love!
When thou shalt look us out of pain,
And one aspect of thine spend in delight[8]
More than a thousand suns disburse in light,
In heav'n above!

REFLECT

What wonders shall we feel, when we shall see
Thy full-ey'd love!

You only have to see a baby's face light up in response to a smile to know the power of a loving look. To see someone's eyes aglow with love for you and delight in you can change you from the inside out. We can spend a lifetime yearning for someone to look upon us in this way.

That is how Christ looks upon us. In this poem Herbert describes the whole of the Christian life, from its beginnings to its consummation in glory, as a response to the Lord looking upon us with love. For now, though, none of us is able to behold the full radiance of the holy love of God. All we can cope with in this life is a "glance." For some of us, it is this glance of love that begins our personal relationship with God. Whether you

6. The harm would have been able to destroy his soul if it had been able to fully accomplish its intent.

7. When Herbert uses "mirth" to describe the effects of God's redeeming love, it means something much stronger than the kind of mild amusement the word signifies today. It is more like sheer joy and delight.

8. "Aspect" is an astronomical term to describe the position of stars and planets. "Glance" and "full" are also astronomical terms. A glance is a mere flash or sliver of light, whereas a "full-eyed aspect" is the full phase of a star, when it shines the brightest.

were raised in a faith-filled home, as Herbert was, or came to know Jesus in other ways, you might well be able to point to a time in your life when you were awakened to a deeply personal faith. Here Herbert refers to a time in his youth when he caught such a glimpse of the radiant love of Christ for him that the joy of it overwhelmed his heart.

In the first flush of our Christian life, there can be an incredibly powerful sense of the presence and love of God, and our response might well be intense and life changing. After that, though, things can get a lot tougher, in life, in faith, in discipleship. We are shaken by circumstances and assailed by doubts. It seems like we don't feel that same kind of love from Christ anymore, and neither is our return of love to him as deep as it was at first. Our walk with God often seems to have more "surging griefs" than "sugar'd delight."

Even so, the power and beauty of that first glance of love from Christ continues to work within us and to carry us through. If the merest glances of love which we receive from Christ in this life can bear us up in the fiercest storms, and win the day over our deepest fears and sorrows, what will it be like when we see him face-to-face?

The term for this is the "beatific vision," and down the centuries theologians have sought to express what it might be like for us to behold God in glory. Herbert turns that around, and I think he is exactly right. He asks us instead to reflect on what it will be like to experience *Christ beholding us* with the full radiance of his love, brighter than the light of a thousand suns, and no longer just in occasional glances. We will experience his "full-ey'd love" for all eternity, a love that will "look us out of pain."

SCRIPTURE: REVELATION 21:3–4

DWELL

- Which words, images, or phrases from the poem stand out to you? Ask the Holy Spirit to speak to you through them.
- What thoughts, feelings, or actions are prompted in you as you bring the poem and the Scripture text into conversation with each other? Hold these promptings before God.
- Has there been a time in your life when you felt newly awakened to the love of Christ? Give thanks for that experience and allow this reminder of it to strengthen you in your life of faith now.

- What difference might it make as you are going through hard times in your life and your faith to keep hold of the knowledge that Christ looks upon you with love?
- Go back to the final stanza, and Herbert's ecstatic anticipation of what it will be like to experience the fullness of Christ's love for us when we see him face-to-face—a love that will take away all our pain, and shine more brightly than the light of a thousand suns. Spend time simply letting your heart and mind and soul dwell with the deep and dazzling love of the Lord for you.

PRAY

Be thou my vision, O Lord of my heart;
naught be all else to me save that thou art.
Thou my best thought by day or by night,
waking or sleeping, thy presence my light.

High King of heaven, my victory won
may I reach heaven's joys, O bright heaven's sun!
Heart of my own heart whatever befall
still be my vision, O Ruler of all.[9]

GOING FORWARD

Notice—and give thanks for—the work that God has been doing in you through this poem. Be attentive to any next steps God might be inviting you to take.

9. This prayer consists of the first and last stanzas of Eleanor H. Hull and Mary E. Byrne's translation of the hymn "Be Thou My Vision": https://hymnary.org/text/be_thou_my_vision_o_lord_of_my_heart.

Aaron

Although this is a poem about Herbert's priestly calling and identity, it translates readily for all of us as we reflect on our calling to live as disciples of Jesus.

Holiness on the head,
Light and perfections on the breast,
Harmonious bells below, raising the dead
To lead them unto life and rest:
Thus are true Aarons drest.[1]

Profaneness in my head,
Defects and darkness in my breast,
A noise of passions ringing me for dead
Unto a place where is no rest:
Poor priest, thus am I drest!

Only another head[2]
I have, another heart and breast,
Another music, making live, not dead,
Without whom I could have no rest:
In him I am well drest.

1. Exodus 28 gives a description of the clothing for Aaron as high priest. See especially Exodus 28:30 for the urim and thummim (meaning light and perfection) on the breastplate, verses 33–35 for the golden bells on the hem of his robe, and verses 36–38 for the plate engraved with "Holy to the Lord" to be fastened on the turban.

2. For Christ the head, see, e.g., Colossians 1:18.

Christ is my only head,
My alone-only heart and breast,
My only music, striking me ev'n dead,
That to the old man I may rest,
And be in him new-drest.[3]

So, holy in my head,
Perfect and light in my dear breast,
My doctrine tun'd by Christ (who is not dead,
But lives in me while I do rest),[4]
Come people; Aaron's drest.

REFLECT

Come people; Aaron's drest.

If we're honest, we all recognize the distance between how we wish things were in our attempts to live for Christ and the reality of how things actually are. Herbert expresses that here in terms of what it means for him to be a parish priest, but all of us can connect with what he says. And all of us need to hold onto the same grace-filled truth that Herbert holds out for us here: that who we most truly are is rooted in our being clothed with Christ.

This poem's title and clothing imagery come from a rather obscure part of Scripture: the detailed description of Aaron's high priestly vestments (the special clothing of his office) in Exodus 28. The Geneva Bible, which was the most popular household Bible before the King James Version of 1611 (and still for some time afterwards), has a drawing of Aaron in his vestments, with marginal notes describing what some of his garments signified. It is likely that Herbert had this picture in the back of his mind.

For all that the first stanza depicts how "true Aarons" are dressed, we also know from the episode of the golden calf (Exodus 32) that not even Aaron himself could truly live up to the meaning of his clothing and his office. There is something oddly encouraging about that for us. As the letter to the Hebrews explains, it is Jesus Christ himself who is our true and perfect High Priest. We are clothed with Christ in our baptism (Galatians 3:27), and then, by the Spirit, for the rest of our lives we are in the process

3. For the death of the "old man" (old self) and being newly clothed in Christ, see e.g., Romans 6:6; Galatians 3:27; Ephesians 4:20–24.

4. These lines (and also the previous stanza) call to mind Galatians 2:20, where Paul says that it is no longer he who lives, but Christ who lives in him.

of putting off our sinful self (the "old man" mentioned by Herbert [Romans 6:6–11]) and putting on Christ and his righteousness (e.g., Romans 13:14; Ephesians 4:22–24).

Mostly we think of being clothed with Christ as a rich metaphor, but it's easy to imagine Herbert reflecting on these themes as he put on his vestments in preparation for leading worship. It is only because Herbert knows he is clothed with Christ that he can accept his calling. He struggled with his call to ministry for many years. In an earlier poem, "The Priesthood," his sense of unworthiness emerges as one of the main reasons for his hesitation. That hasn't disappeared, but now Herbert is able to recognize that there is no such thing as being "worthy" of his calling, and also that it isn't all about him. Above all, it is about Christ, who lives in him and is at work through him. Herbert helps us to come to the same kind of realization about ourselves and our life of discipleship too.

The very structure of the poem beautifully encapsulates all of this. Did you notice that the final word of each line is the same for each stanza: head, breast, dead, rest, drest? With those words, Herbert takes us from the ideal that not even Aaron could live up to, to his very flawed self, to seeing his identity and calling transformed in and by Christ. The same pattern works for each of us too. This is a brilliant poetic rendering of the idea that Christ's righteousness becomes ours, and the truth that we are *simul justus et peccator*: at once justified (set right with God) and sinners. It also helps us to grasp something of what it means to say with Paul that it is no longer we who live but Christ who lives in us (Galatians 2:20).

This is very good news for all of us! We will never be flawless Christians, any more than Herbert could be a perfect priest, but that doesn't stop us from seeking to love, serve, and follow Christ. This isn't an excuse for complacency. Like Herbert, we remain acutely aware of how far we fall short. But we also trust that we are clothed in Christ's righteousness, and that even amid our "defects and darkness" Christ is alive in us, re-tuning us, and accomplishing his purposes through us.

SCRIPTURE: ROMANS 6:5–11

DWELL

- Which words, images, or phrases from the poem stand out to you? Ask the Holy Spirit to speak to you through them.

- What thoughts, feelings, or actions are prompted in you as you bring the poem and the Scripture text into conversation with each other? Hold these promptings before God.
- Although it can be uncomfortable, we need to be honest about the ways we fall short in our walk with Christ. Be as specific as Herbert is here in naming some of those in prayer, knowing that Christ is our great and merciful High Priest who understands our struggles.
- While we do need to confess our sins, we can sometimes feel overwhelmed by the distance between the kind of person we ought to be and the kind of person we are. Receive this poem's reminder that you are in Christ, that Christ is at work in you, and that he is your righteousness, sanctification, and redemption (1 Corinthians 1:30).
- Let your imagination play with the metaphor of clothing. What does it mean for you to be "clothed with Christ"? How might you "get dressed" each day with that in mind? In what ways do you still need to grow into your Christ clothes?

PRAY

Loving Lord Jesus, our great High Priest,
with you alive in me, and me alive in you,
I know that I do not need to fear.
Clothed in your righteousness
I can seek to live fully for you now,
and then boldly approach the eternal throne
for the crown that will be mine through you.[5]

GOING FORWARD

Notice—and give thanks for—the work that God has been doing in you through this poem. Be attentive to any next steps God might be inviting you to take.

5. I wrote this prayer based on the final stanza of Charles Wesley's hymn "And Can It Be, That I Should Gain": https://hymnary.org/text/and_can_it_be_that_i_should_gain.

The Elixir

This is one of Herbert's most straightforward poems. We might not immediately grasp all the words and images, but we get the point. As always with his "simple" poems, though, there is more going on than we might realize. From the title to words like "tincture" and the reference to "the famous stone / That turneth all to gold," Herbert is drawing on the ancient "science" of alchemy here, which was still very much practiced in his time. As we saw when we reflected on "Easter," the discovery of the philosopher's stone would lead to the perfection of physical and spiritual matter and also the elixir of eternal life. "Well," says Herbert in this poem, "we have something even better than that!"

Teach me, my God and King,
In all things Thee to see,
And what I do in anything
To do it as for Thee.

Not rudely, as a beast,
To run into an action;
But still to make Thee prepossest,[1]
And give it his perfection.

A man that looks on glass,[2]
On it may stay his eye;
Or if he pleaseth, through it pass,
And then the heav'n espy.

1. "Still" meant always in Herbert's time. These lines are about always pausing to bring our actions to God, rather than simply rushing thoughtlessly onto the next thing.

2. No one is exactly sure what Herbert has in mind here! Most likely the "glass" is a mirror, but it could also mean a window. Very possibly Herbert wants us to think of both!

All may of Thee partake:
Nothing can be so mean,[3]
Which with his tincture—"for Thy sake"—
Will not grow bright and clean.

A servant with this clause
Makes drudgery divine:
Who sweeps a room as for Thy laws,
Makes that and th' action fine.

This is the famous stone
That turneth all to gold;
For that which God doth touch and own
Cannot for less be told.

REFLECT

For Thy sake

Sometimes it can feel like we're never doing enough for the Lord, can't it? Or that we're not doing spectacular-enough things. Maybe we look around at church and see people who seem to be involved in so much and doing so many good things. Maybe we scroll through social media and see the stories of the amazing work some people are doing. And we think, "Am I a failure? Why can't I manage to do these kinds of things for God and the church and the world?"

Most of us live our lives as very ordinary people, doing very ordinary things. Our days go by in a haze of routines, and we sometimes wonder, where is God in all of this? And does anything I do really matter? The things that fill our days can seem so unimportant that we have no idea how they could be of much significance to anyone, let alone God.

Friends, this is our poem! It is a prayer asking God to help us to live our ordinary daily lives mindful of him at all times and attentive to him in all things. And if we do, says Herbert, the alchemists can down tools. We have something far better than they are seeking. Here is a way to transform all the very ordinary things of our lives into what is far more precious than gold: awareness of the presence of God, and the fellowship with God that leads to eternal life.

3. "Mean" signifies lowly, menial.

I don't know about you, but I need to hear this—and pray this kind of prayer—over and over again. Finding God in the ordinary is incredibly important because this is where our discipleship mostly happens. As Tish Harrison Warren puts it, "God is forming us into a new people. And the place of that formation is in the small moments of today. . . . The crucible of our formation is in the anonymous monotony of our daily routines."[4]

What if we allowed "The Elixir" to teach us to pray without ceasing (1 Thessalonians 5:17)? This doesn't mean spending all your time on your knees with your eyes closed. It means: "Teach me, my God and King, / In all things thee to see, / And what I do in anything / To do it as for thee." What those opening lines are seeking—to be able to see God in all things, and to do all things for him—is both incredibly simple and incredibly difficult, as all of us know who have attempted to do them consistently. This is "the practice of the presence of God."[5] The rest of the poem shows us different ways to do just that.

What if, rather rushing on to the next thing (or mindlessly making our way through our to-do list) we took some time to pause and bring God into what we're up to?

What if everything we see could become a lens to show us something of God, and the ordinary stuff of our lives could become a window to reveal the presence of God to us?

What if, by the Holy Spirit, even our most menial, boring, ordinary tasks, done for the Lord's sake, might be transformed into the gold of a place of encounter with the living God?

SCRIPTURE: COLOSSIANS 3:17

DWELL

- Which words, images, or phrases from the poem stand out to you? Ask the Holy Spirit to speak to you through them.

4. Warren, *Liturgy of the Ordinary*, 21, 34.

5. This is the title of the classic little book, readily available in many editions, based on the sayings and letters of Brother Lawrence (c. 1614–91). It is all about learning to be attentive to God in the ordinary tasks of life, based on Brother Lawrence's experiences working in the kitchen and then as a sandal maker in a monastic community.

- What thoughts, feelings, or actions are prompted in you as you bring the poem and the Scripture text into conversation with each other? Hold these promptings before God.
- Consider memorizing Colossians 3:17 and the first stanza of this poem and allowing these words to lead you toward what it might mean to "pray without ceasing."
- Do you feel like you are on autopilot most days? Are you running flat out? Does it seem like you're missing out on the present moment because you're always thinking about the future? Try to practice the discipline of pausing to bring your plans and the items on your to-do list before God. Listen for what God might have to say about them.
- Ask the Holy Spirit to help you to be particularly attentive to the presence of God through what you see and do this week.

PRAY

Fill thou my life, O Lord my God
in every part with praise;
praise in the common words I speak,
life's common looks and tones.
So shall no part of day or night
from sacredness be free
but all my life in every step
be fellowship with thee.[6]

GOING FORWARD

Notice—and give thanks for—the work that God has been doing in you through this poem. Be attentive to any next steps God might be inviting you to take.

6. This prayer is taken from Horatius Bonar's hymn "Fill Thou My Life, O Lord, My God": https://hymnary.org/text/fill_thou_my_life_o_lord_my_god.

Death

This poem begins the remarkable closing sequence in which Herbert deals with the "last things," traditionally death, judgment, heaven, and hell. Herbert subverts our expectations for all of them, beginning with this rather lighthearted poem addressing death. Herbert doesn't sugarcoat death's awfulness, but because of Christ we know that the final outcome is glorious resurrection life.

Death, thou wast once an uncouth hideous thing,
Nothing but bones,
The sad effect of sadder groans:[1]
Thy mouth was open, but thou couldst not sing.[2]

For we considered thee as at some six
Or ten years hence,
After the loss of life and sense,
Flesh being turned to dust, and bones to sticks.[3]

We looked on this side of thee, shooting short;[4]
Where we did find
The shells of fledge souls left behind,[5]
Dry dust, which sheds no tears, but may extort.[6]

1. Death is the sad outcome of a person's grievous dying groans.

2. Herbert is picturing a slack-jawed skull.

3. "For we considered thee . . . bones to sticks" means that our image of death is based on what a body is like years after being buried—a skeleton.

4. We come up short in our thinking about death because we consider it only in earthly terms ("this side") rather than from the perspective of the final resurrection.

5. A skeleton is like the shell of a soul that has "fledged" (flown to heaven). When we die, our souls are with the Lord, awaiting their reunion with our resurrected bodies.

6. Dust cannot weep, but it can wring ("extort") tears from others.

But since our Saviour's death did put some blood
Into thy face,[7]
Thou art grown fair and full of grace,
Much in request,[8] much sought for as a good.

For we do now behold thee gay and glad,
As at dooms-day;[9]
When souls shall wear their new array,
And all thy bones with beauty shall be clad.

Therefore we can go die as sleep, and trust
Half that we have[10]
Unto an honest faithful grave;
Making our pillows either down, or dust.[11]

REFLECT

And all thy bones with beauty shall be clad.

Would you rather not have to think about death? If so, you are not alone. Ours is a culture of death denial and death avoidance, very much including a tendency to hide death away in institutional settings. People in Herbert's time came face-to-face with death and dying from early childhood onwards. Without the kinds of medical interventions that are possible now, death was an ever-present risk and reality, meaning that everyone in the seventeenth century was far more intimately aware of it than most of us today. When people who know death far better than us choose to write like this about it, we'd do well to listen. We might end up with a healthier attitude toward death than our culture—even our church culture—tends to offer us.

Herbert doesn't shrink from the ugly reality of death. Seen in and of itself, it is a hideous thing, and dying is hard. We groan our way painfully into it. Before long, our bodies become a pile of bones, and our flesh disintegrates into dust.

7. Christ's death has put some color back into death's cheeks!

8. "Much in request" means often requested.

9. Dooms-day is the last day—the return of Christ in glory, with the resurrection of the dead and the final judgment.

10. The "half that we have" is our bodies (in contrast to our souls).

11. If we sleep our pillow will be feather down; if we die our pillow will be the dust of the grave.

This is part of the truth about death, and we need to acknowledge it, but it is not the whole picture. This is simply what death looks like after earthly years reduce our bodies to skeletons. We need to see death from the perspective of doomsday, when our lowly bodies will be transformed to be like Jesus' glorious body (Philippians 3:21). Jesus' resurrection is the foretaste of the joyous celebration to come, when, as our Scripture text for this poem tells us, we will not be less clothed (in other words, we will not merely be immortal souls) but will be even more fully clothed than we are now, for we will be dressed in our glorified resurrection bodies.

All of this means that we can confront the brutal reality of death honestly, and also that we do not need to fear it any more than we fear sleep. When death comes, we can surrender half of ourselves (our bodies) to the grave, knowing both that our souls will be with the Lord and also that when the day of resurrection comes there will be the unutterable joy of eternal life in bodies that are radiant with a beauty that will never decay or fade.

SCRIPTURE: 2 CORINTHIANS 5:1–5

DWELL

- Which words, images, or phrases from the poem stand out to you? Ask the Holy Spirit to speak to you through them.
- What thoughts, feelings, or actions are prompted in you as you bring the poem and the Scripture text into conversation with each other? Hold these promptings before God.
- Knowing that you are gently held by the Lord, reflect with him on your experience of death so far. How has this shaped your attitude toward death? Share the thoughts and feelings that arise in you with the Lord who loves you, who endured death for you, and who has triumphed over it for you.
- It can be hard to hold together the grim reality of death with the truth that it is also the gateway to eternal life with the Lord. Which side of death do you tend to emphasize most? How might you acknowledge the truth of both, as Herbert does here?
- In Herbert's time there were many resources to help people to prepare for death, spiritually and practically. The genre was called *ars moriendi* (the art of dying). In our culture of death avoidance, we

could do with something like the equivalent today.[12] Spend some time thinking about how you might prepare for the inevitability of death. What practical things need to be put in place? What might it mean for your discipleship to live more intentionally in the awareness that your physical death is coming, and so is the fullness of eternal life?

PRAY

Lord of life,
we entrust to your merciful keeping
those who have died.
For our bodies now,
we know that it is a case of
earth to earth, ashes to ashes, dust to dust,
but in you we have a sure and certain hope
of the resurrection to eternal life
through your mighty power
when on the Last Day
you will change our lowly bodies
to be like your glorious body.
For this we give you thanks and praise.
Amen.[13]

GOING FORWARD

Notice—and give thanks for—the work that God has been doing in you through this poem. Be attentive to any next steps God might be inviting you to take.

12. One place to start might be Billings, *End of Christian Life*.

13. I wrote this prayer to echo the committal prayer that Herbert would have known in the 1662 BCP.

Dooms-Day

We would expect this poem to be about the last judgment. Even the title implies that: "doom" here means judgment. But Herbert saves that for the next poem. Here, he deals with what comes first: the return of Christ and the resurrection of the dead. Herbert can't wait! Rather astonishingly, he is also having fun! He is parodying love poems, imagining the risen dead getting dust in their eyes, and cracking some rather macabre jokes. Behind all of this, though, is a poignant question: Why is it taking so long for Christ to come back and set everything right?

Come away,
Make no delay.
Summon all the dust to rise,
Till it stir, and rub the eyes;
While this member jogs the other,[1]
Each one whisp'ring, *Live you brother?*

Come away,
Make this the day.
Dust, alas, no music feels,
But thy trumpet:[2] then it kneels,
As peculiar notes and strains
Cure Tarantula's raging pains.[3]

1. Member here can mean either a body part or a person (a member of the body of Christ); "jogs" means nudges.

2. Our dead bodies cannot hear or respond to any music except the trumpet on the last day.

3. The sound of the trumpet cures death, just as dancing to the music of the tarantella (an Italian folk dance) was supposed to cure people from the bite of a tarantula spider.

Come away,
O make no stay![4]
Let the graves make their confession,[5]
Lest at length they plead possession:
Flesh's stubbornness may have
Read that lesson to the grave.[6]

Come away,
Thy flock doth stray.
Some to winds their body lend,
And in them may drown a friend:[7]
Some in noisome vapours grow
To a plague and public woe.[8]

Come away,
Help our decay.
Man is out of order hurl'd,
Parcelled out to all the world.[9]
Lord, thy broken consort raise,[10]
And the music shall be praise.

REFLECT

Come away,
Make this the day.

What are your thoughts and feelings about the return of Jesus? Have you experienced teaching that has made you dread the prospect of it? At the

4. "Make no stay" means do not delay.

5. "Let the graves acknowledge that they have no legal right to the bodies."

6. Our human stubbornness might have taught the grave to want to keep hold of our bodies. After all, possession is nine-tenths of the law, as the saying goes!

7. The idea here is that the dust of our dead bodies ends up being carried away on the winds of a storm, the very storm that could cause a friend to drown.

8. Rotting bodies give off harmful fumes ("vapours") that cause disease.

9. Human beings are in a state of total disorder; we are in pieces and all over the place, both metaphorically and, once we are dead, literally.

10. A "broken consort" refers to a group of musicians playing a mixture of instruments. Herbert wants the Lord to bring together the whole consort of the redeemed to enable them to play music to his praise (and the term "raise" also points to how church music in Herbert's time was set to a higher pitch than other music). But "broken" also has connotations of sinfulness, and "consort" is also another word for spouse, so Herbert is also longing for the time when the broken, sinful spouse of Christ (the church and all of its members) will be raised to glory.

very least, the return of Christ in glory and the resurrection of the dead are usually treated with great solemnity and awe. Herbert is having none of this!

For a start, he tries to persuade Jesus to hurry up by borrowing a phrase from love poetry. "Come away" is what a lover says to his beloved, urging her to make haste to come with him and surrender to his advances. Herbert borrows this phrase not only from secular love poetry but also the Song of Songs (2:10, 13 KJV) and uses it to urge Christ to return. He is taking up the cry of "Maranatha" ("Come, Lord!" [1 Corinthians 16:22]), and the prayer for him to come quickly at the end of Revelation (Revelation 22:20).

And then there is the way that he portrays the newly risen dead, rubbing their eyes as if after a long sleep, and because of all the swirling dust caused by the resurrection! They are also nudging each another, whispering excitedly, "Are you alive too?!" The word "member" could refer to each believer as a member of Christ's body (1 Corinthians 12), but since the word also means a body part, it is also as if a leg were saying to a foot, "Is that you?! Are we connected again?!" With that we're taken to the valley of dry bones with the question "Can these bones live?" and all of them coming back together (Ezekiel 37).

Amid all the quirkiness, though, there is real urgency. Herbert articulates what so many of us feel too: there is so much death, decay, and brokenness in the world, and Jesus is taking a very long time to come back and sort everything out. As Herbert jokingly points out, Jesus has left the dead bodies in their graves for so long that the graves might claim the right to keep them. What's more, the accumulating dead bodies are becoming a health hazard to the living.

Herbert isn't just longing for the wonder of the resurrection. He is also aching for the coming restoration of all things. Behind this poem is the scriptural question "How long, O Lord?!" When will all the brokenness and discord in our lives, in the church, in the world, be replaced by the glorious music of eternal joy and praise? Herbert has no answers, but he joins his voice with the people of God down the ages in this playful but also deeply earnest plea, "Come, Lord Jesus!"

SCRIPTURE: 1 CORINTHIANS 15:51–57

DWELL

- Which words, images, or phrases from the poem stand out to you? Ask the Holy Spirit to speak to you through them.
- What thoughts, feelings, or actions are prompted in you as you bring the poem and the Scripture text into conversation with each other? Hold these promptings before God.
- Are you one of the many people who have been taught to fear the return of Jesus? Herbert longs for it because he knows it will usher in the fullness of redemption, when sin and death will be no more, and everything broken will be made whole. What difference does dwelling on these themes make to how you envisage Jesus' return?
- We believe in the bodily resurrection, but we often picture eternal life merely in terms of being immortal souls. Let Herbert's excitement about the resurrection here and in the previous poem help you to delight in the glorious future that God has for your body, and let this reminder of how much your body matters to God help to shape your attitude toward it now.
- What circumstances in your life or the life of those you love, in your country or in the world, prompt you to ask "How long, O Lord?" and to yearn for the time when Christ will return to set all things right and make all things new? Hold these before God, as you join Herbert in praying, "Come, Lord Jesus!"

PRAY

Lord Jesus Christ,
we long for your coming in glory
when you will consummate
the victory you have won
over sin and death.
We long for you to bring
the dawning of the last day,
when truth and right will triumph

over lies and wrong,
with endless joy and bliss
for us and all creation.
Hear your people as we pray,
Come quickly, King of Kings!
Amen.[11]

GOING FORWARD

Notice—and give thanks for—the work that God has been doing in you through this poem. Be attentive to any next steps God might be inviting you to take.

11. I wrote this prayer based on John Brownlie's hymn "The King Shall Come When Morning Dawns": https://hymnary.org/text/the_king_shall_come_when_morning_dawns.

Judgement

After cheerfully dealing with death and then urging Jesus to hurry up and come back, Herbert is about to surprise us again. He begins this poem on the last judgment with a sense of terror, as we might expect, but he ends very unconventionally indeed. He is witty and almost impudent as he envisages what he will do when he comes before the throne—and he is also absolutely right!

Almighty Judge, how shall poor wretches brook[1]
Thy dreadful look,
Able a heart of iron to appall,
When thou shalt call
For ev'ry man's peculiar book?[2]

What others mean to do, I know not well;
Yet I hear tell,
That some will turn thee to some leaves therein[3]
So void of sin,
That they in merit shall excel.

But I resolve, when thou shalt call for mine,
That to decline,
And thrust a Testament into thy hand:
Let that be scann'd.
There thou shalt find my faults are thine.[4]

1. To "brook" means to bear or endure.

2. "Peculiar" means particular. For the "books" at the last judgment, see Revelation 20:12.

3. "Leaves therein" signifies pages in the book of their life.

4. A testament is a legal document, but here he means the Bible, and especially the New Testament, which shows that all his sins have been laid upon Jesus, who has borne the penalty of them for him.

REFLECT

There thou shalt find my faults are thine.

Has the last judgment been presented to you in absolutely terrifying ways? You might well have read books or experienced preaching and teaching that have used the prospect of the last judgment to try to frighten the hell out of you. You might also be able to call to mind "last judgment" scenes in art, with a stern-faced Christ consigning the people on his left to hell. If you know classical music, you might be able to hear in your mind's ear the fearful settings of the "Dies Irae" (The day of wrath) in Mozart's *Requiem*, for example, or Verdi's.

And then we have Herbert! Once again, he turns the usual approach upside down, and he is scripturally and theologically spot on as he does so. And once again, he is having some holy fun with the last things!

Herbert wonders how any of us "poor wretches" will be able to face the prospect of the book of our life being opened before Christ the Judge on the last day. Perhaps some people might be able to point to enough sinless pages to be saved? Very wisely, though, he's not going to try that! The instant the Judge calls for the book of his life, he is going to thrust a copy of the New Testament into his hand instead, because on that basis his acquittal is assured! Slam dunk!

Could there be a bolder, wittier, and more scripturally sound last judgment–move than that? And could there be a more wonderful way to remind us of the true basis of our salvation?

Whatever some people might think, none of us will have any purely sinless pages in the book of our lives, and there is nothing about us that would "merit" salvation. It is not that how we live our lives is irrelevant, or that we can never do anything worthwhile. The New Testament itself makes clear that we should expect our faith to bear fruit in our lives, and that what we do in this life matters, including for the last judgment. It is simply that nothing we do could ever be the basis of our salvation. That rests in Christ alone, who has borne the penalty for our sins and restored us to loving communion with God.

All of this means that, like Herbert, we do not need to be afraid of the last judgment. Our confidence can never be in ourselves, but we can have all the confidence in the world in Christ and what he has done for us. There truly is no condemnation for those who are in Christ Jesus (Romans 8:1). As the twentieth-century Reformed theologian Karl Barth put it, he is the Judge judged in our place.

SCRIPTURE: ROMANS 8:31–39

DWELL

- Which words, images, or phrases from the poem stand out to you? Ask the Holy Spirit to speak to you through them.
- What thoughts, feelings, or actions are prompted in you as you bring the poem and the Scripture text into conversation with each other? Hold these promptings before God.
- Have you found yourself terrified by the thought of the last judgment? Let Herbert's holy boldness help you to rest in the assurance that you do not need to be afraid, and that you can place your whole trust in Christ.
- When we do not fear future judgment, we are set free to live more fearlessly into our faith now. Knowing that our salvation depends on Christ, not us, we can hear the call to live more fully for him without worrying about being "good enough." With this in mind, how might you live more boldly into what it means for you to be a faithful follower of Jesus?
- When we are no longer afraid of the last judgment, we do not need to be afraid of what the book of our life contains. We also do not need to wait until the last day to look over it with Christ! Consider setting aside some time to practice what is sometimes called a "life review." Reflect back over your life so far with Christ in prayer. Be attentive to where the Holy Spirit prompts you to pause and explore more deeply; and to times in your life when you sense God's affirmation or challenge; and to what the Spirit might be teaching you for your walk of faith going forward.

PRAY

God of all grace,
we thank you that you sent your Son, Jesus,
to break the power of death
and bring life and immortality to light
through the gospel.

He shared our life,
took upon himself our death,
and opened the kingdom of heaven
to all believers.
Look not on us:
but look on us as found in him,
and bring us safely through the judgment
to the joy and peace of your presence.
Amen.[5]

GOING FORWARD

Notice—and give thanks for—the work that God has been doing in you through this poem. Be attentive to any next steps God might be inviting you to take.

5. This prayer comes from the First Order for a Funeral Service in the Church of Scotland's *Book of Common Order*, 255.

Heaven

Herbert is about to subvert our expectations again! Rather than attempting to go into detail about what heaven or eternal life will be like, he gives us an echo poem, where the last syllable of one line becomes the only word of the next. This was a very popular kind of poetry in his time. While it might strike you as rather weird, stick with it. Herbert is asking questions you might want to ask too.

O who will show me those delights on high?
Echo: *I.*
Thou Echo, thou art mortal, all men know.[1]
Echo: *No.*
Wert thou not born among the trees and leaves?
Echo: *Leaves.*[2]
And are there any leaves, that still abide?
Echo: *Bide.*
What leaves are they? impart the matter wholly.
Echo: *Holy.*
Are holy leaves the Echo then of bliss?
Echo: *Yes.*
Then tell me, what is that supreme delight?
Echo: *Light.*
Light to the mind: what shall the will enjoy?
Echo: *Joy.*

1. In Greek mythology, Echo was a mortal nymph who was cursed by her unrequited love for Narcissus, so that she could speak only by repeating the last words spoken to her. She eventually faded away until only her voice remained. As Herbert is at pains to point out, this poem's divine Echo is not at all like that mythical Echo!

2. Rather than the leaves of the trees and groves where nymphs lived, the leaves here are the pages of Holy Scripture with their abiding truth.

But are there cares and business with the pleasure?
Echo: Leisure.
Light, joy, and leisure; but shall they persever?[3]
Echo: Ever.

REFLECT

O who will show me those delights on high?

Have you ever wondered not just about what heaven is like but how we can really know anything about it? Herbert's opening questions have a surprisingly contemporary ring to them. Who can tell us what it is like "on high"? And can we trust the answers that the Echo gives, if all it is doing is repeating our words back to us? In other words, the daring question behind the questions here is: Are we just making all of this up? Is the idea of heaven just our own cosmic wish fulfillment? Is what we think of as the voice of God just us talking to ourselves?

And the answer the Echo gives is: No, we aren't making all this up. Our very limited words really do point to heavenly reality, and in the pages (leaves) of Holy Scripture God really is giving us access to abiding truths, but in ways that respect the limits of our language and our capacities. John Calvin says that the way God communicates with us in Scripture is similar to how a mother or a nurse speaks in baby language to an infant. That is not so far from how the divine Echo is answering the questions here, in simple words, one word at a time.

These single-word answers end up offering a surprisingly rich summary. While Scripture doesn't give us many answers to our questions about heaven and eternal life, it gives us "the echo of bliss"—just a hint of the wondrous reality that awaits us. Our supreme delight will be in the Light of God. There will be no need for the sun, for God and the Lamb will be our light (Revelation 21:23; 22:5). The redeemed, too, will shine like the sun (Matthew 13:43), and our minds will be enlightened so that we know as we are known (1 Corinthians 13:12), comprehending all that can possibly be grasped of the being and the love of the triune God. As a result, there will be nothing but eternal, overflowing, ever-increasing joy.

But will we still be anxious and busy there, as we are here? No! says the Echo. There will be leisure. As you read that word, think of the promised

3. While we would now say "persevere," with the accent on the last syllable, in Herbert's time the accent of "persever" fell on the second syllable, which is why it rhymes with "ever."

rest of Hebrews 4:9–11, and also of "recreation." In Herbert's day, only a very tiny, very wealthy proportion of the population had any significant "leisure time." The promise of eternal "leisure" would have been an almost unimaginable luxury to most: time to be and to do in richly good and fruitful ways rather than the endless grind of anxious toil in order to survive.

As Herbert says, a blissful life of light, joy, and leisure sounds amazing . . . but will it last? Oh yes, says the divine Echo. Forever.

SCRIPTURE: PSALM 16:9–11

DWELL

- Which words, images, or phrases from the poem stand out to you? Ask the Holy Spirit to speak to you through them.
- What thoughts, feelings, or actions are prompted in you as you bring the poem and the Scripture text into conversation with each other? Hold these promptings before God.
- Unless we can trust that Scripture is holy—that it is from God—and that in it we can discover what is abidingly true, how can we believe what it says about things that are so far beyond what we can know? Give thanks to God for the gift of Scripture and consider ways that you might continue to deepen your knowledge of and love for it.
- What questions do you have about heaven and eternal life? If you would like some help to continue to think about these questions, look for scripturally rooted resources rather than accounts of "near-death" experiences of going to "heaven" and coming back. Bear in mind, too, that much of what we can come up with is simply "sanctified speculation" because Scripture doesn't give us many details. We won't know until we get there!
- Bliss, delight, light, joy, pleasure, leisure . . . These are some of the words Herbert gives us to begin to build up a picture of eternal life with the Lord. We could add many more! Prayerfully write your own list of words and phrases that evoke for you something of what eternal life will be like.

PRAY

Holy and loving triune God,
we can hardly begin to imagine
the joy, the radiant glory, the bliss
of eternal union and communion with you
in the company of all your people!
What feasting, what rejoicing,
what blessed rest, what jubilant song,
what unutterable love there will be!
Help us to live now in ways that fit us
for our eternal life to come with you,
one God, Father, Son, and Holy Spirit,
forever and ever.
Amen.[4]

GOING FORWARD

Notice—and give thanks for—the work that God has been doing in you through this poem. Be attentive to any next steps God might be inviting you to take.

4. I wrote this prayer based on a poem by the medieval monk Bernard of Cluny, best known in the translation of J. M. Neale as the hymn "Jerusalem the Golden": https://hymnary.org/text/jerusalem_the_golden_with_milk_and_honey.

Love (III)

This is the final poem in the main section of *The Temple.* It is also the final poem in Herbert's "last things" sequence, and he upends our expectations one more time! We have had death, the return of Christ, and the resurrection, judgment, and heaven. Now we have . . . not hell but love, as divine Love himself welcomes Herbert in, takes him by the hand, and leads him to the feast.

Love bade me welcome: yet my soul drew back,
        Guilty of dust and sin.
But quick-ey'd Love, observing me grow slack
        From my first entrance in,
Drew nearer to me, sweetly questioning,
        If I lack'd any thing.

A guest, I answer'd, worthy to be here:
        Love said, You shall be he.
I the unkind, ungrateful? Ah my dear,
        I cannot look on thee.
Love took my hand, and smiling did reply,
        Who made the eyes but I?

Truth Lord, but I have marr'd them: let my shame
        Go where it doth deserve.
And know you not, says Love, who bore the blame?
        My dear, then I will serve.
You must sit down, says Love, and taste my meat:
        So I did sit and eat.

REFLECT

Love bade me welcome

Friends, hear Herbert's last words to you: You are beloved.

This is Herbert's most famous poem, and his most beautiful. It is also one of the easiest for us to understand, and one of the richest for us to dwell upon.

At the end of our spiritual journey with Herbert, we can see that the love of God in Christ has been his spoken and unspoken theme in every poem. Sometimes he has been aware of it. Sometimes not being able to feel God's loving presence has plunged him into desolation. Other times he has sought to flee from God's love. Often his sense of unworthiness has made it extremely difficult for him to accept that God could possibly love him. Many times, he has tried to earn or deserve God's love in some way. Much of that complex mix is present in this poem. Much of that complex mix describes us and our walk with God too.

Through all the ups and downs of his faith journey, this saving love has been the truest and deepest thing he has known about God and about himself. And knowing himself as he does, that is why Herbert assumes that this is also true for all of us who read his poetry. If God can love him so dearly and so deeply, then that is how God loves you too. That is why Herbert wants Love to be his—and above all, God's—last word to us in this central collection of poems in *The Temple*.

In his manual for pastors, Herbert describes how a pastor might come alongside those who are in spiritual despair, fearing that God has rejected them. He speaks of how the pastor "dives into the boundless ocean of God's love" with them. He shows them that God loves everything that he has created, very much including them, because how could the perfect Artist hate anything that he has made? And his love for them as a sinner is even greater than the love with which he created them, because out of that love he came as Love incarnate to overcome all that separates them from his love. Only by utterly despising that Love, says Herbert, can we shut ourselves out. It is only thrusting away his arm that prevents us from being embraced by God.[1]

Even when Herbert tries one last time in this poem to turn away from Love, Love's infinitely gentle patience and persistence (and wry humor!) win out. The deeply beautiful tenderness and wondrously thoughtful

1. From ch. 34 of Herbert's *A Country Parson*, in Tobin, *George Herbert*, 256.

attentiveness of the perfectly loving Host ensure that his guest finally feels wholly welcome, utterly loved, and completely at home.

Do you remember how, in "The Glance," Herbert anticipated the overwhelming holy awe of Christ's full-eyed love in eternity, more radiant than a thousand suns? He isn't quite ready for that here, but quick-eyed Love immediately notices what this particular beloved guest needs. Frozen at the threshold, crushed by his sense of unworthiness, Herbert doesn't need dazzling light. Like so many of us, he needs loving intimacy. So Love comes close, and just as Jesus so often does in the Gospels, asks what he would like. It all comes pouring out: Herbert's sense of being hopelessly unworthy and unlovable, and yet, in his exclamation, "Ah my dear . . . !" we see all of his love and longing too. With unutterable tenderness, Love responds by taking his hand. As we have seen many times, this is the gesture that, throughout Herbert's poetry, most intimately signifies Christ's love for him.

Even when he finally accepts that he is indeed loved and welcome, Herbert still cannot quite allow himself simply to be a beloved guest: "My dear, then I will serve!" Ever so gently, Love is having none of that. In this life we are indeed called to love and serve God and others as our response of gratitude for all that we have received from God. But this poem is a glimpse into the fullness of our redemption, when Jesus promises that we will recline at his table, and he himself will serve us (Luke 12:37). Like the younger son in the parable (Luke 15:11–32), we will be welcomed home not as servants but as the beloved children we are, with the table set for a feast.

And so, in one last mic-drop final line, and after so many poems reflecting his struggle to accept that he is beloved of God, and to allow himself to be a recipient of God's grace, we have Herbert's expression of complete surrender.

In the meanwhile, there is another table to which we are lovingly welcomed by our dear Host, as a foretaste of the coming marriage feast of the Lamb. Herbert loved the Lord's Supper with every fiber of his being, so it is no surprise that this depiction of coming home to Love also points us to the communion table. Let Love bid you welcome to this table, until that day when he will welcome you home to his eternal feast.

SCRIPTURE: 1 JOHN 4:16–19

DWELL

- Which words, images, or phrases from the poem stand out to you? Ask the Holy Spirit to speak to you through them.
- What thoughts, feelings, or actions are prompted in you as you bring the poem and the Scripture text into conversation with each other? Hold these promptings before God.
- In this final poem, Herbert is at last able to rest in the experience of being wholly known and wholly loved. Allow yourself to anticipate what this might be like for you. How might this help you to live more freely for Christ now, as you wait for him to welcome you into the fullness of your redemption?
- "Love took my hand, and smiling did reply . . ." Imagine Christ taking *your* hand and smiling at you. What do you feel? And how might Christ reply to your doubts, struggles, and fears?
- Consider taking the time to learn this poem by heart, to let it continue to teach you so much of what you need to know about yourself and about the Lord who loves you.

PRAY

Rather than a prayer, receive this invitation to come into the presence of the Lord:

Come, not because you are strong,
but because you are weak;
come not because of any goodness of your own,
but because you need mercy and help;
come, because you love the Lord a little
and would like to love him more;
come because he loves you
and gave himself for you.[2]

There is no need to hesitate. You are welcome! You are beloved! Come!

2. These or similar words are found in many communion liturgies as the invitation to the table. I have quoted them from the source from which I first heard and loved them, the Uniting Church in Australia's 1980 *Holy Communion: Three Orders of Service*, 31.

GOING FORWARD

Notice—and give thanks for—the work that God has been doing in you through this poem. Be attentive to any next steps God might be inviting you to take.

Bibliography

Andrewes, Lancelot. *The Preces Privatae of Lancelot Andrewes, Bishop of Winchester.* Translated by F. E. Brightman. London: Methuen, 1903.

Anglican Church of Canada. *The Book of Alternative Services of the Anglican Church of Canada.* Toronto: Anglican Book Centre, 1985.

Banyard, Edmund. *Heaven and Charing Cross: A Further Collection of Meditations and Prayers.* Birmingham, UK: National Christian Education Council, 1996.

Billings, J. Todd. *The End of the Christian Life: How Embracing our Mortality Frees Us to Truly Live.* Grand Rapids: Brazos, 2020.

Calvin, John. *Genesis.* Edited by Alister McGrath and J. I. Packer. Crossway Classic Commentaries 25. Wheaton, IL: Crossway, 2001.

———. *Institutes of the Christian Religion.* 2 vols. Edited by John T. NcNeill. Translated by Ford Lewis Battles. Philadelphia: Westminster, 1960.

Church of England. *The Book of Common Prayer.* Cambridge: Cambridge University Press, 2004.

Church of England Archbishops' Council. *Common Worship: Services and Prayers for the Church of England.* London: Church House, 2000.

Church of Scotland. *Book of Common Order of the Church of Scotland.* 2nd ed. Edinburgh: Saint Andrew, 1996.

Drury, John. *Music at Midnight: The Life and Poetry of George Herbert.* Chicago: University of Chicago Press, 2014.

Featley, Daniel. *Ancilla Pietatis: Or The Handmaid to Private Devotions.* London: N.p., 1626.

Guite, Malcolm. *After Prayer: New Sonnets and Other Poems.* Norwich: Canterbury, 2019.

Lawrence, Brother. *The Practice of the Presence of God.* Translated by E. M. Blaiklock. Hodder Classics. London: Hodder Christian Classics, 1981.

McDonald, Suzanne. "George Herbert, the Psalms, and Sabbath." In *Like a Watered Garden: Essays in Honor of Carol Bechtel,* edited by James Hart Brumm, 35–45. Grand Rapids: Reformed Church, 2025.

McKelvey, Douglas Kaine. *Every Moment Holy.* Volume 1. Nashville: Rabbit Room, 2017.

Sibbes, Richard. *Selected Works of Richard Sibbes.* Edited by Alexander B. Grosart. Oxford: Benediction Classics, 2017.

Tobin, John, ed. *The Complete English Poems.* By George Herbert. Penguin Classics. Harmondsworth, UK: Penguin Classics, 1991.

Uniting Church in Australia Assembly Commission on Liturgy. *Holy Communion: Three Orders of Service.* Uniting Church Worship Services. Melbourne: Joint Board of Christian Education of Australia and New Zealand for the Uniting Church in Australia Assembly Commission on Liturgy, 1980.

Warren, Tish Harrison. *Liturgy of the Ordinary: Sacred Practices in Everyday Life.* Downers Grove, IL: IVP, 2016.

Wilcox, Helen, ed. *The English Poems of George Herbert.* By George Herbert. Cambridge: Cambridge University Press, 2007.

www.ingramcontent.com/pod-product-compliance
Lightning Source LLC
LaVergne TN
LVHW100526110826
845146LV00002B/789

9798385262526